The Relationship People

The Relationship People

Mediating Love and Marriage
in Twenty-First Century Japan

Erika R. Alpert

LEXINGTON BOOKS
Lanham • Boulder • New York • London

Published by Lexington Books
An imprint of The Rowman & Littlefield Publishing Group, Inc.
4501 Forbes Boulevard, Suite 200, Lanham, Maryland 20706
www.rowman.com

86-90 Paul Street, London EC2A 4NE

British Library Cataloguing in Publication Information Available

Library of Congress Cataloging-in-Publication Data

Names: Alpert, Erika R., 1981- author.
Title: The relationship people : mediating love and marriage in twenty-first century Japan / Erika R. Alpert.
Description: Lanham : Lexington Books, [2021] | Includes bibliographical references and index. | Summary: "The Relationship People examines the marriage industry and its clients in neoliberal Japan. It addresses what industry professionals are promoting to ease Japan's low rates of marriage and childbirth, what singles are actually doing, and whether focusing on introducing more singles to each other can effectively solve Japan's millennial woes"— Provided by publisher.
Identifiers: LCCN 2021040227 (print) | LCCN 2021040228 (ebook) | ISBN 9781498594202 (cloth) | ISBN 9781498594226 (paper) | ISBN 9781498594219 (epub)
Subjects: LCSH: Marriage brokerage—Japan. | Dating services—Japan. | Marriage—Japan. | Single people—Japan.
Classification: LCC HQ802 .A47 2021 (print) | LCC HQ802 (ebook) | DDC 306.810952--dc23
LC record available at https://lccn.loc.gov/2021040227
LC ebook record available at https://lccn.loc.gov/2021040228

For the now absent, but always beloved Serenity, the best feline coauthor any writer could ever ask for.

And for my partner, Elliott, who, as they say in Russian, is like a stone wall for me to lean upon.

And for my mother, who divorced when I was in my teens and whose affection for 90s personal ads probably set me down a lifelong path of scholarly inquiry. I am fortunate that she has supported me upon it in love, joy, and perplexity for all the years since.

And for her mother, my grandmother, of blessed memory, who did so much to make sure that following the path of research and discovery was materially accessible to me, from childhood through my early adulthood, and whose love and guidance I carry with me always.

Contents

Acknowledgments

No work on this scale is possible without the generosity, cooperation, guidance, and at times, indulgence, of any number of people and institutions. The research discussed in this monograph covers a time period from 2007–2019, and I am astounded at the amazing support I've received from so many different people over those twelve years—let alone the help I've received during the terrible years of 2019–2021, in which the support of others has been especially appreciated. There are many, many people to whom I owe debts that can never be repaid, but at the very least, I can attempt to account for their contributions here.

Let me start with the humans. Most particularly to be thanked is my PhD advisor, Bruce Mannheim, for his guidance over the long haul of my graduate training, his intellectual insight, emotional compassion, vast patience, and continued friendship. I also owe tremendous thanks to Maria Lepowsky, who has been the advisor of my assistant professorship, and who is the reason this book exists at all. My editor, Kasey Beduhn at Lexington Books, also appeared at exactly the time I was talking to Maria, to ask if a particular conference paper was part of a larger project, and would I perhaps like to turn that project into a book? And I did. Daniel Pugh, my (former) dean, and Gavin Slade, my department chair at Nazarbayev University, have been amazingly patient cheerleaders. Sofia An, my late friend and former department chair, never let me believe for a second I couldn't finish this project. I also owe a debt of deep gratitude to Paul Manning and Sabina Perrino for giving me feedback on my proposal and helping me to shape this book into its current form. My partner, Elliott Bowen (historian and author in his own right) supported me in countless material and immaterial ways, but in particular, took on a fair amount of domestic labor to give me time to write. Let us also never discount the power of takeout for helping academic work get done. Thank you to the Eco-Shop on the first floor of my building and Koktem Café in Nur-Sultan (Astana), for being so close by and so very delicious.

The data in any anthropological work is generously gifted to the anthropologist from those who are willing to let them into their work and their lives. In Kyoto and Osaka, I need to thank Nakanishi Keiji and Kiyomi, along with their daughters Sayuri and Yumi, for never being less than wonderful, welcoming, and willing to share. I also most particularly need to thank Kawakami-sensei and Takamiya-sensei, whose warm welcome back in 2007 made my research seem possible in the first place. These wonderful matchmakers and friends let me into not only their business lives, but into their homes and families, showing me through multiple kinds of practice the happiness that matchmaking can and does bring into the lives of its practitioners and clientele, as well as the everyday labor that makes it all possible. I am endlessly thankful for the kindness of Yuko Iwasaki and the staff of Green e Books in Kyoto, for giving me a home away from home, and a place where I could always go to talk about relationships and compare attitudes about life, the place of love, and what our relationships mean with some of my closest Japanese friends. My conversations there did much to situate what I learned from matchmakers in a larger cultural context. The bookstore was closed shortly before I received my PhD, but I can see its spirit of cultural exchange living on in all of our future projects and current travels. Many, many thanks must also go to Esther Ahronheim, whose help was invaluable in parsing out everyday life in Kansai over the course of a couple summers and my eventual move to Kyoto long-term. Finally, researching online dating meant spending more time in the Tokyo area, which gave friendships old and new a wonderful chance to blossom. Thank you to Nishaant Choksi, Patrick Galbraith, Keiko Nishimura, Shunsuke Nozawa, Junko Teruyama, and Rika Yamashita for providing such a wonderful intellectual base for me in Tokyo and pointing me in so many useful directions; and to Roy Berman, who is just awesome. Thank you also to the staff of Diverse and Recruit, both companies who produce online partner matching platforms, for teaching me a bit about this business from the creation and marketing side.

A book also never instantaneously becomes *a book*, but lives several lives in advance as dissertation chapters, abstracts and conference papers; pieces of journal articles that somehow got written too; half-finished manuscripts, and piles of supplementary data from research assistants. So, let me thank those research assistants, and let me also say that the students I have met at Nazarbayev University are truly the best I've had the privilege of teaching and working with in my life. Nurdana Adylkhanova and Assel Shlykova helped me tremendously with early, lightly quantitative research on Zexy Enmusubi profiles. Makhabbat Boranbay and Tamarakhonum Davlatova gamely ventured into the broader world of online dating and application affordances for me, trawling through the scholarly literature and also documenting profile creation processes on every site they could get their hands on. And, finally, Zhannur Dildabayeva and Maral Nuridin ventured onto Japanese government websites to dig up all manner of white papers and policy documents for me. All of you lightened my research burdens tremendously, and Makhabbat's own research on Tinder in Kazakhstan really challenged me and helped me to crystallize my own ideas. Thank you all for the privilege of letting me witness your transition from students to independent researchers and colleagues, and maybe help it along a little bit, in the course of my own project.

Numerous conferences gave me the opportunity to present advance versions of my work, or to think through related issues. I need to thank Nishaant Choksi (again) for encouraging me to apply for the inaugural Conference on Asian Linguistic Anthropology in Siem Reap, Cambodia, in 2019; to Anna Bax for organizing a fantastic panel on digital sexualities at the American Anthropological Association Annual Meeting in 2017; to Ilana Gershon for having me on an equally fabulous panel about mediated conversation and neoliberal subjectivities at the inaugural meeting of the Society for Linguistic Anthropology in 2018, and to my former colleague Alex Miltsov (now at Bishop's University) for organizing a workshop in our department at NU on digital research methods.

On top of all the personal support that sustains large-scale scholarly work, these projects also require institutional support and funding. I wish to extend my most profound gratitude to the ITO Foundation for International Education Exchange for their financial support of my fieldwork; without their belief in my project, none of this would have been possible. Additional financial support during my graduate education came from the Center for Japanese Studies at the University of Michigan, the Department of Anthropology, and the Department of Linguistics. Thanks are also due to the staff of the Inter-University Center for Japanese Language Studies in Yokohama, and through them, the Shoyu Club, who were of great assistance with my language studies as well as with smoothly transitioning me from those studies into my fieldwork. The Center for Research in Humanities at Kyoto University gave me an intellectual home during my fieldwork between 2009–2011 and my advisor there, Masakazu Tanaka, provided comments and feedback on some of my earliest research results. My experiences in seminars there were also invaluable in helping me negotiate the complicated balancing act of participation versus observation. At Nazarbayev University, I've been grateful for research startup funds via the Social Policy Grant program, and additionally I am pleased to have been awarded a Faculty Development Competitive Research Grant (No. 090118FD5331). These two funding schemes, along with additional travel funds from the Department of Sociology and Anthropology, helped me through much of my summer fieldwork between 2015 and 2019.

Finally, I think no warning can quite prepare anyone for the emotional dramas of fieldwork and the subsequent, and different, emotional drama of reifying the fieldwork experience in text form and presenting it to a wider audience for criticism and comment. I have been truly blessed with friends around the world who have been there for me—in person, in text message, in IM and email, and sometimes even on the phone—at every new and challenging stage of this project, and without whom I am certain I would have lost my mind. I love you and thank you with all my heart, especially my writing group and Lexi Temple. To my family: thank you for your constant support, belief in me, countless care packages, and willingness to let me run halfway around the world (multiple times) to follow my passion for research. And finally, thank you to my father, who always wanted me to be a scholar.

Notes on Names

With the exception of the Nakanishi family, who have given me permission to use their real names, and the name of their organization, the Japan Matchmaker Organization (Nihon Nakōdo Kyōkai), all names that appear in this ethnography have been changed. Minor personal details have also been changed in order to protect research participants from being reidentified. However, I have typically given a pseudonymous personal name for people whom I knew as such, and a pseudonymous family name for others. Where a full name is given, the name is listed in the Japanese order, with family name first, and personal name second.

The usual form of address in Japanese is a person's family name, for people whom one is not particularly close to, followed by the common honorific suffix –*san*, which is approximately equal to Mr./Ms./Mx. in English. The personal names of closer acquaintances are followed by any number of suffixes indicating status and social distance (or lack thereof)— or the lack of any suffix at all, which is its own kind of indicator. The most common of these is again –san, and thus my Japanese friends typically call me Erika-san (with the diminutive suffix –chan or the shortened form Eri reserved for a few best friends). Although it is not universal, many matchmakers address each other as –sensei, "teacher," a term of respect used not only for literal teachers, but also for respected professionals in other fields (such as doctors or lawyers). I have opted to use this honorific to distinguish the matchmakers who appear in the following pages from other people, outside the matchmaking industry, who have nonetheless contributed their perspectives to my research. Thus, matchmakers are usually referred to as Surname-sensei, with Name(-san) or Surname(-san) denoting friends, acquaintances, and research participants who are not matchmakers.

Notes on Transcription and Translation

For maximum readability for English speakers, I have used a modified Hepburn system for transliterating Japanese. For those who are not familiar with how Japanese is typically pronounced, please find a detailed guide below.

- Single consonants have more or less typical English values, except "r," which conventionally represents the alveolar flap (the "t" in "water," for American English speakers; the "r" in "very" if you are stereotypically "very very" British). The other outlier is "f," which is pronounced with lips nearly closed, instead of with the top teeth against the bottom lip.
- Doubled consonants (pp, mm, tt, ss, nn, ssh, tch, kk) represent "long" consonants, in which the consonant is pronounced for twice as long, two beats instead of one.
- A consonant followed by "y" represents a palatalized consonant, pronounced as a single unit, not as two syllables. (E.g., "Kyoto" is two syllables, not three.)
- "N" at the end of a syllable is moraic, that is, one beat in and of itself. Where a moraic "n" (ん) *precedes* a syllable beginning with a vowel or a "y," it is offset by an apostrophe to indicate that it is not part of the following syllable. Thus, じぶん (自分) becomes "jibun," and あんぜん (安全) is "anzen," but れんあい (恋愛) is rendered as "ren'ai."
- Vowels have roughly the value you might expect in Spanish, Italian, or Latin, although "u" is pronounced with flat, rather than rounded, lips.

- Japanese has a distinction between long and short vowels (e.g., "kuki" means a "plant stem," but "kūki" means "atmosphere"). Long vowels are just what they sound like: they are pronounced for literally twice as long. Long ā, ō, and ū are represented with a macron above the vowel. Long ī is represented by a doubled vowel, as in "iikata." Long ē has long been conventionally represented in English as "ei" (e.g. "sensei"), which is used here as well. In most cases, this mirrors Japanese orthography where え (e) is followed by い (i) to represent length. Where the Japanese orthography has a doubled "e" instead of "ei," I have used a macron, as in "onē-san." Where vowels are doubled (other than ii), this signals that they are not actually pronounced as a single long vowel, as in "baai."

Finally, I wish to note that this is by no means a discourse or conversation analytical work. Quotes from observations and interviews are presented in English only, unless there are features of the original Japanese that require explicit presentation and discussion. Representation of pauses and prosody through punctuation is approximate. Sentence-final punctuation, commas, and hyphens represent the approximate intonation curve and length of pause. Longer pauses are represented with an ellipsis. Where Japanese text is presented at length, it is given in Japanese orthography and then in English translation. In translation, I have attempted primarily to be faithful first to the sense of things, as it is very difficult to approximate some of the stylistic differences between English and Japanese with anything remotely approaching a good parallel in translation (and at any rate, I am not a literary translator). Where stylistic differences or other features of the original are consequential for interpretation, they are noted explicitly in the surrounding text.

Permissions

Thank you to President Nakanishi Keiji of the Nihon Nakōdo Kyōkai for permission to use his personal name, and the name of his organization, in this work. Thank you also to Vice President Nakanishi Kiyomi for permission to use her name as well. The Nakōdo Kyōkai has been so central to my research from 2010 onwards that I can hardly imagine not giving them credit here for the education they so generously bestowed upon me.

Additionally, portions of the data and arguments in this book were previously published in the following articles:

Alpert, Erika. 2014. "Stoicism or Shyness? Japanese Professional Matchmakers and New Masculine Conversational Ideals." *Journal of Language and Sexuality* 3 (2): 191–218. https://doi.org/10.1075/jls.3.2.02alp.

———. 2020. "The Role of Dating Site Design in Gendered Self- Representation and Self-Animation in Online Japan." *Journal of Asian Linguistic Anthropology* 2 (4): 67–79. https://doi.org/10.47298/jala.v2-i4-a4.

1

✛

Introduction

Love's Labors and Laborers

I am not very good at writing ethnographic vignettes. Linguistics was my first discipline; I came to anthropology later, in graduate school. Its narrative techniques have always been a little foreign to me. They slip through my fingers, whereas grammar has a nice way of staying put for analysis. But anthropology is not a comfortable science for its practitioners, and it doesn't really allow us to ever stay still, in a familiar spot. So let me begin by telling you, dear reader, about how I went on dates for science. Two, actually—no more, no less. And they were not, strictly speaking, "dates" in the English sense of the term. They were *omiai*, a Japanese term that literally means "see and meet," and which describes the formal first meetings of prospective heterosexual marriage partners that have historically been arranged for young singles by parents and go-betweens. The first one took place earlier in my studies, and I met my match in Kyoto, which afforded me some privacy. The second one, however, took place in Osaka, whose urban hotels are omiai hotspots on the weekends, and where most of the matchmakers in a given hotel lobby would have at least known me by sight, if not by name and reputation.

It was 2010, and I was supposed to meet a country doctor who was in town for a conference. One of my most deeply impressed memories of this event was begging Kawakami-sensei, my matchmaker, friend, research participant, and teacher, to please find an out-of-the-way hotel where no one would see *me*, the *researcher*, in the role of the *client*. This felt horrifyingly urgent to me, in spite of the fact that throughout most of my research into matchmaking and online dating, my positioning as a potential client, as a relatively young, single woman capable of experiencing matchmaking for myself, was central to how matchmakers treated me. Later, it was a key part of how I developed rapport with friends and acquaintances who talked to me about their online dating practices. There is inescapable entanglement and tension in being two kinds of scholar, and in being both a subject and an object of research. I have always wanted to separate out my selves into clear roles, but it's not possible, and I don't know how it could be.

Perhaps you have anticipated that this story is a metaphor, dear reader. It is a metaphor for the many topics entangled in my research itself, in the context of my research, and in my own being as I inhabited and conducted this research, situated between the United States (where I am from), Japan (which has been the focus of my research life since 2005), and Kazakhstan (where I have been based as a scholar since 2014). This is a book about contact and connection, about the ways we form relationships—or perhaps more importantly, about the ways we are *encouraged* to form relationships, and about the kinds and qualities of contact deemed *good* or *productive* or *helpful* in terms of securing individual happiness through human connection, along with the specific social benefits tied to those particular connections called "marriage" (*kekkon*, in Japanese).

This book is also about the many ways that having intimate relationships feels impossible for many people around the world. Specifically, it is about concrete economic factors like low wages and long working hours that are a buzzkill at best, and a socially destructive force, at worst. Moreover, it is about economic philosophies that give ultimate responsibility to individuals and their personal efforts, who subsequently have only themselves to blame for their failures if they cannot stay afloat on low wages and long hours, or meet expected life-course milestones like marriage, parenthood, and financial independence. While Japanese singles have fewer resources available to them now than previous generations, and less stability, these life-course milestones have remained in much the same places as before. Alternative family forms, including cohabitating and childbearing outside of marriage, have yet to achieve much social acceptance. Ronald and Alexy warn us that, rather than shifting family styles, in Japan we see "indications that processes of family formation are breaking down or, for many, not happening at all," but perhaps this is because families are "changing form and function and many people cannot imagine any other shape than the existing one" (2011, 13–15). Emma Cook notes that while, in theory, irregular and precarious labor could open up new imaginaries of gender and family, in practice, most irregular laborers "have a sense of failure about their inability to live up to marital ideals embedded in mainstream understandings of manhood" (2019, 179).

Finally, to the extent that this is a book about marriage, and the industries that have cropped up to try and help single people enter into this connubial state, this is a book about gender, sexuality, and specifically, straight people. While an increasing number of municipalities in Japan are recognizing same-sex partnerships in some form or another, marriage still remains the exclusive province of straightness, despite the decision of the Sapporo District Court in March 2021, which declared that marriage laws that exclude same-sex marriages are unconstitutional (Terahara 2021). Whether the Diet will make changes to Japanese marriage laws based on this ruling is an open question, as is how the marriage industry might respond. Khor and Kamano (2021) point out that Japan uses its own self-proclaimed history of sexual tolerance, paradoxically, to take same-sex marriage and LGBTQ+ visibility off the table as a viable political option, and note that arguments in favor of same-sex marriage often serve to further entrench (primarily heterosexual) marriage as natural and normal, compared to other modes of family formation or intimacy.

And indeed, an alarming number of people, straight and otherwise, who assume that heterosexuality is a force of nature, that it "just happens" if men and women are in sufficient proximity to each other. But it turns out that heterosexual relationships like marriage are not natural outcroppings of normal human sexual and pair-bonding urges, sprouting like mushrooms after rain. Rather, they are deliberately built. They require resources and support. And where those resources and support are lacking, marriage rates will go down. This is a problem, insofar as marriage and divorce rates are believed to say something about the health, happiness, and stability of a given society. It is also a problem insofar as heterosexual marriage is still tightly linked to childbearing, particularly in Japan. Children are, of course, The Future. A drop in marriage rates can make demographers feel like time-travelers watching themselves vanish from photos, as their antics in the past prevent their own future births.

In sum, this is a book about The Relationship People: the people at work in Japan building those straight relationships, doing the social labor of making connections, setting up communication infrastructure, both face-to-face and high-tech, and evaluating the resources to hand for making those connections "official." I borrow this term from the Japanese word *nakōdo*, which means "matchmaker" or "go-between," but which is written with the characters for "relationship" (仲) and "person" (人). These are the people committed to making heterosexuality happen. Some of them are professionals, some are amateurs laboring on their own behalf using online dating platforms, and some are in-between: working as matchmakers part-time, helping out friends, and seeing if they can't learn something themselves in the process. I came to know them through their websites, their blogs, and their books, and through professional matchmaking associations like the Nihon Nakōdo Kyōkai ("Japan Matchmaker Association," hereafter NNK for short). I came to know them through friends, and friends of friends. And I came to know them because, in my way, I was one of them. All of these different "relationship people" are negotiating tensions that pull them in opposite directions. Kawakami-sensei's marriage and business partner, Takamiya-sensei, always described matchmaking as a business that "doesn't make any money" (*mōkaranai*), and yet, it's a business they've been at for at least twenty years. This is, in and of itself, a nice metaphor for the situation of many Japanese singles, most of whom want to get married one day, even if it's a goal that often feels impractical or impossible because there's no time, because there's no money, and because they never seem to meet anyone interesting.

Writing about practices like online dating and matchmaking also has a seemingly obvious appeal, since "geosocial networking apps"—location-based apps like Tinder or Grindr that help match people for purposes from casual sex to finding a soulmate—are becoming, have already become, an ever-present background activity in this brave new world where computers with attached cameras and microphones live in our pockets. (In 2010, in the middle of my dissertation fieldwork, I had only just acquired my very first iPhone; it was life-changing.) You, the reader, might reasonably ask why I chose to study these processes in Japan, given that so many of them are global. You might also very reasonably ask why I focus on the connection of online dating—a comparatively new phenomenon—to revivals and reinventions of older practices like matchmaking. There are several reasons. The first is that Japan has now suffered low and lower birth rates for decades. While societies around the world are aging, Japan is aging faster, and has been aging for longer. Solutions to Japan's demographic woes have proved elusive—at least within the scope of what its governments and businesses have been willing to try. In this context, Japan's marriage and online dating industries explicitly bill themselves as a potential tonic for low birth rates. The NNK site aimed at recruiting new matchmakers describes the benefits of the job as "being able to bring happiness to people," and "contributing to society."[1]

However, when we examine the factors surrounding Japan's long-standing birth and marriage-rate crisis, it becomes plain that Japan suffers from late capitalist phenomena that closely mirror those in other developed countries, surrounding the politics of demographics, the structure of labor, and, in a very real and big sense, the question of what we owe each other as kin and as members of a society. This book is an attempt to disentangle one strand of an elaborate braid made out of ethnonationalist sentiment; ideas about masculinity, femininity, and the family; the role of extended kin groups; late capitalism and its failures; neoliberalism and its effects on what we believe individuals to be responsible for; and the way that we, as humans, form enduring connections with each other amid all this. This strand of the braid—the development and popularization of professional matchmaking and online dating—has been given its shape by the way it is interwoven with all of these other phenomena, and with the cultural specificities of Japan, where this story is set. However, I think that the way these concepts are elaborately plaited together will sound familiar to many readers. In this introduction, my goal is to briefly lay out four strands of these entwined phenomena, with reference to insights about "connection" from linguistic anthropology, and discuss the role they play in Japan's matchmaking industries. From there, I lay out the substance of the rest of this book, and discuss the research process that lead me to this data and these conclusions. For Japanese readers and other scholars of Japan, I hope this story sounds familiar. For readers from elsewhere, I hope you hear echoes of this story in your own experiences.

STRAND ONE: LANGUAGE AND CONNECTION

The spring of 2008 in Japan brought with it a new fad: "marriage hunting" (*kekkon katsudō*, or *konkatsu* for short). Individuals who take up the call to konkatsu, or facilitate others' konkatsu projects through careers in the marriage industry, do much of this labor through language, in part because most of this labor happens online. And because most of this labor happens online, the language used is specifically textual communication.[2] Language is the means through which matchmakers advertise and advise, through websites and blogs and books. It is the means through which they care for their clients, through text messages and emails. Likewise, language is the means through which online daters compose profiles, and through which singles get to know each other, through conversations in dating apps, messaging apps, and sometimes even in-person. Language is one of the primary means of "self-presentation": the self-interested display of personal qualities in interaction, as per sociologist Erving Goffman's (1959) definition. As if anticipating the focus on self-responsibility in all things that neoliberal capitalism would bring the workers of the world, Goffman's concept of self-presentation imagines selves as constant theatrical performances, constantly working to determine their own meaning through *consistent* performances over time. His analytical focus on the self and the performance team in the workplace, and on the performances of hoteliers and salespeople toward guests and clients, presages the model of the self as a business. Gershon (2014) describes the neoliberal self as a brand that must be sold in the process of seeking employment. "Self-presentation" in profiles and texts and blogs and books is how we forge ourselves into those brands and sell them.

If interactions between singles can be described as a marriage market (and they often are), then profiles are the advertisements, created by

matchmakers for their clients, and by users of online partner matching
services for themselves. Being largely, although not exclusively, written
texts, they can be analyzed as such, using the tools of linguistic anthropology. Linguists and anthropologists interested in the social aspects of
language have developed systems to recognize and describe different
kinds of variation in language (word choice, grammatical forms, pronun-
ciation, etc.), while paying close attention to the *social meanings* of different language forms. This can involve noting how speakers or writers use
different linguistic forms to create a variety of meanings or personae in
media production or face-to-face interaction. It can also involve attention
to "metapragmatic" commentary, that is, explicit talk about language use
and variation, and what people believe they mean. Examples of this kind
of metapragmatic commentary might include konkatsu website FAQs con-
taining advice on how to write profiles, send messages, and use the site.
Such documents tell users what kind of language is "good," "effective," or
"engaging"—what kind of language will lead to the desired result of establishing communication with someone that leads to a marriage. Another
example would be the advice that matchmakers give their clients on how
to interact with each other when meeting or dating a prospective marriage
partner. While regular in-person dates are essential, Nakanishi Kiyomi,
the vice president of the NNK, advises other matchmakers in educational
seminars that they should counsel clients to keep up regular messaging
habits between dates. Even a lone heart emoji can help to maintain the
open channel of communication necessary for a couple to get to know
each other and establish a foundation for deciding whether to marry. This
is metapragmatic commentary: telling us how communication should or
shouldn't work, within any particular cultural system.

Ultimately, metapragmatic beliefs in any given social world serve as a
system of evaluating people according to their language use. Although
metapragmatic assessments of language use affect all domains of social
life, in the case of matchmaking and online dating, users apply metapragmatic knowledge at all stages of a relationship, from browsing profiles
to introductions, to dating and long-term communicative behavior, in
order to judge whether a person is interesting or not, compatible or
not, engaged in the relationship or not, in love—or not. If we return to
Nakanishi-sensei's seminars on how to counsel dating couples, we will
find that she maintains that the main reason clients break up instead of
getting married at this stage is because at least one of the partners has
failed to make their feelings clear. In other words, there's a communicative breakdown. If individuals are being tasked with new kinds of interpersonal labor to brand and market themselves in order to succeed at
both work and interpersonal relationships, metapragmatic assessments of
linguistic habits are how participants in the marriage industry determine

whether other people are doing a good job. This is the jumping-off point for this ethnography: the place where linguistic behavior and neoliberal models of the marketable self meet. What kinds of labor are Japanese matchmakers and singles engaging in, and does it seem to be working? Is it leading to relationships? Is it creating romance? Is it creating belonging? Ultimately, metapragmatic evaluation of other people's language is often how we determine whether we get along with someone; whether we feel loved, appreciated, or wanted; whether we feel like we belong in a relationship or a group.

In this sense, metapragmatic analysis of different individuals' language use can tell us who we believe to have a rightful place in society and who does not, or whether we are meeting our obligations to each other. For example, Alexy (2011) examined the shifting metapragmatics of how married couples address each other in neoliberal Japan. For prior generations, standards of mutual or affectionate address for couples emphasized each others' positions in the family—"mother" or "father." But now, using "mother" as an affectionate term of address implies, not love between equals, but a relationship based on dependence that feels tremendously uncomfortable to anyone invested in a more individualistic paradigm. Neoliberal models of romance insist on the free union of independent partners, and terms of address and endearment are understood as signs pointing to how husbands and wives conceptualize their relationship to each other. Alexy addresses this metapragmatic issue by examining the claim that the "wrong" (kin-oriented) terms of endearment are increasingly a cause of divorce in Japan (where divorce rates are on the rise). In the presence of kin-oriented terms of endearment, heterosexual marriages are now perceived to be at risk of falling apart, rather than being held together by complementary roles within the family. Such language is now understood to produce troublesome disconnection instead of facilitating closeness and emotional expression within a marriage. In a related fashion, this book explores the linguistic labor that people engage, in an attempt to facilitate connection instead of disconnection; social belonging and appropriate transitions to adulthood instead of lingering in awkward singleness; and relationships that are ultimately meant to contribute to stabilizing society and to reproduce the Japanese nation and culture, in the wake of decades of severe demographic threat.

STRAND TWO: ETHNONATIONALISM
AND THE POLITICS OF DEMOGRAPHICS

This might seem like a dramatic jump from the previous topic, but it is not, to the extent that marriage and reproduction are central to the survival of ethnonationalist states. Worldwide, populations are aging as fewer children are born, although there are some places where this process began earlier, and is proceeding more dramatically (United Nations, Department of Economic and Social Affairs, Population Division 2019). Japan, with its long lifespans, low marriage rates, and low birth rates, is one of the most dramatic cases. *Shōshika* (少子化), the "change to few children," commonly translated as "low birth rate," is a widely recognized problem. Although historically in Japan, marriage was more or less universal for all men and women (Cornell 1984), marriage rates have long-since fallen, with research going back well over twenty years (Raymo 1998). But despite knowing about this problem, it only seems to be worsening. Japan's birth rate hit a new all-time low in 2019 (Jozuka, Yeung, and Kwan 2019), and then again in 2020 (Kyodo News 2021).

In the face of these existential threats, we see a worldwide rise in ethnonationalist responses. In the United States, right-wing, white nationalist violence is on the rise, and far-right political parties have been scoring victories worldwide. The UK's Brexit vote is a dramatic example of the effects of right-wing activism, and other countries are seeing a shift to the right politically, including Japan and other countries throughout the Asia-Pacific region (Chako and Jayasuriya 2018). All of this can be seen as part and parcel of a "global crisis of democracy" (530). Opportunities for immigration and asylum for refugees, whether they be Hispanic or Muslim, is everywhere contentious, as one of the most explicit goals of nationalists is to reserve national territory and social participation exclusively for citizens. This goes hand-in-hand with a more narrow definition of who is entitled to be a citizen. In the United States, full national belonging has racial, religious, and linguistic restrictions. Barreto and Lozano (2017) analyze the historical case of the naturalization of Puerto Ricans to discuss the way that race, ethnicity, and language complicate the question of whether American citizenship is primarily "civic" or "ethnic." They argue that in practice, US citizens occupy different "tiers" of citizenship, with Anglo-Saxons historically possessing the realest real citizenship, as compared to members of other ethnic groups. This question is not merely historical, as, at present, Hispanic and Muslim citizens and migrants to the United States face "frightening levels" of "the wholesale criminalization of immigrants" (Hayduk and García-Castañon 2018, 309).

By comparison, in India, nationalism is ethnically, religiously, and linguistically Hindu. Niraja Gopal Jayal (2019) discusses the move to lineage-based (*jus sanguinis*), ethno-religious models of citizenship throughout India's history, with amendments to its Citizenship Act that have covertly, then directly, targeted Muslims for exclusion from citizenship, while creating exceptional rules to fast-track migration of Hindus from Pakistan. China has now waged a years-long campaign of terror and genocide against its Muslim minorities, particularly ethnic Uyghurs in Xinjiang, seeking to bolster this "internal colony" against external influences that, ironically, it must open up to in order for the success of China's Belt and Road Initiative to revitalize trade across Asia (Hayes 2019). To return to Japan, citizenship is ethnically and linguistically Japanese—not indigenous Ainu, not life-long resident Korean, and definitely, *definitely* not immigrants (see especially Siddle 2010, who focuses on Ainu issues). Although practical realities and recent changes to Japanese law will allow for greater numbers of immigrants, Japan has a long history of having "one of the strictest immigration regimes in the OECD world" with a mere 2 percent of the population consisting of foreign migrants (Hollifield and Sharpe 2017, 374).

Anti-immigration sentiment tends to presuppose a particular order of gender and family, for if the national community cannot be expanded or perpetuated by welcoming immigrants, then the fate of the nation rests on the biological reproduction of ethnically, religiously, or racially desirable citizens. Anti-abortion sentiment in the United States is quite frankly about the control of reproduction, with the constitutional right to an abortion now threatened by the extremely conservative makeup of the Supreme Court (Gostin, Parmet, and Rosenbaum 2020). New, harsh laws are criminalizing abortion providers (Narayana et al. 2019), as well as even being used to prosecute women who lose pregnancies under other circumstances (e.g., Bates 2019). Progress for transgender rights that has seen expansion of gender categories and flexibility in many developed countries (Taylor, Lewis, and Haider-Markel 2018) has met with a backlash that also can be seen as part of the desire to control reproduction. P. Miller et al. (2017) argue that both disgust at transgender bodies and authoritarian sentiments play into rejection of transgender rights. This all makes perfect sense. If biological reproduction is an ethnonational imperative, then biological definitions of gender, and gender roles focused on people with uteruses as women and mothers, must remain in place—or be forcibly instituted. This, despite the fact that a clear biological definition of "sex" is not readily forthcoming from actual sex biologists. According to Carpenter (2016, 74), shame and definitional difficulties make it hard to count the prevalence of intersex conditions, but they affect anywhere from 0.5–1.7 percent of all humans. Freedom to manage one's body, whether that involves access to birth control, abortion, or gender-affirming medical care, is generally antithetical to national demographic purity—if, indeed, such a thing has ever existed, or would be desirable if it could exist.

Japan is somewhat different, at least insofar as anti-immigration policies have long been the norm; there is no "crackdown" on immigration. Targeted immigration programs in the past that sought to import more palatable migrants have become national and international embarrassments. The case of Brazilian Japanese is one of the most well-known. From 1990, changes to immigration law in Japan made it possible for the descendants of Japanese migrants to Brazil to "return" to Japan, given shared Brazilian-Japanese and Japanese understandings that Japanese cultural traits had been preserved in Brazil, and were transmitted by shared Japanese blood. To the surprise of both parties, upon migration to Japan, Brazilian-Japanese migrants turned out to be culturally different after all. The Japanese reaction to these co-ethnic yet *different* migrants was disappointment, along with attempts to discourage and limit immigration from Brazil (Tsuda 2001). By 2009, in the face of a global recession, the Japanese government began offering to pay Brazilian-Japanese migrants to go home, which was, plainly, not Japan. Immigration-averse Japan has also looked to technology to help its shrinking population labor as much as in the past, even with fewer people. Robertson (2007) explicitly ties anti-immigration sentiment in Japan with the rise of its robotics industry, arguing that robots are meant to prop up conservative visions of family and nation.[3]

At the same time, various government programs have attempted to stimulate the birth rate, largely unsuccessfully. Takeda (2008) argues that neoliberal policies in Japan that center the individual and try to place men and women on equal economic footing are perhaps doomed, because children require care. Therefore, the Japanese economy requires not just the redistribution of labor between men and women outside the home, but also inside. However, the government has mostly aimed to commercialize care work, and various government programs are "strikingly silent about male participation in care work" (206). Therefore, in Japan's post-Fordist system, where workers earn wages meant to support an individual, rather than a whole family, women tend to put off marriage and childbearing rather than dealing with the inequalities in care work that still exist in Japanese social life, or attempting to pay for commercial childcare services. The ability of individual women to solve their problems personally through individual avoidance of marriage and childbearing, however, has arguably hampered their ability to fight collectively for government policies and social change that would meaningfully transform gender relations to the extent needed to raise the birth rate (Schoppa 2010).

STRAND THREE: GENDER,
THE FAMILY, AND THE OBLIGATIONS OF KIN

Beginning in the 1970s (Takeda 2008, 198–199), Japan's demographic shift to less marriage, later marriage, and fewer children has quite necessarily altered the definition of "adulthood" as well as widespread understand-ing of "men's" and "women's" roles. At one point "adulthood" and "mar-riage" were practically synonyms. However, feminist sociologist Ueno Chizuko noted as far back as 1987 that this strong association between adulthood and marriage had been well and truly undone. In addition to the lower rates of marriage, it's also important to note that fewer people are entering into relationships of any kind. The gap between "married" and "single" in Europe and North America is filled by various kinds of "in a relationship," or "living together." Such relationship statuses are "single" in the strict sense of "not married," but carry a certain degree of social recognition and respect nonetheless, and most people in such a relationship would probably not describe themselves as "single." But in Japan, demographically single is much more likely to correspond with being actually on one's own, without a romantic or domestic partner of any kind. Although the number of Japanese women who report ever experiencing cohabitation is rising compared to the past, it is still much lower than it is in much of Europe and North America (Raymo, Iwasawa, and Bumpass 2009). And new Japanese social taxa, such as the category of *ohitorisama*, or "singletons," rather than legitimizing nonmarital rela-tionships, try and put a positive spin on singleness instead—women's singleness especially, because this is particularly stigmatized. "Ohito-risama" generally describes women who are content on their own, and have sufficient economic resources to sustain a comfortable solitary lifestyle, even though this is not actually achievable for many of Japan's unmarried women (Dales 2014).[4] This further bears on the question of reproduction because illegitimacy is still rare and socially unaccepted in Japan (Hertog 2009). At least a full third of new marriages can be con-nected to unplanned pregnancies, in an attempt to avoid the stigma of unwed parenthood (Raymo and Iwasawa 2008). So the more singletons, the fewer children.

So why are Japanese singles not marrying, and not reproducing bio-logically or culturally? Arguably, the current state of capitalism, which emphasizes individual over corporate responsibility, has induced levels of precarity that actually disincentivize heterosexuality. The reflex of this phenomenon in the United States has often been characterized as mil-lennials "killing" industries associated with traditional adulthood mile-stones: marriage, home ownership, diamond purchases (Paul 2017). To phrase this more academically, in Japan, "adult transitions have become increasingly fragmented and non-linear" (Ronald and Izuhara 2016, 391), in the absence of secure adult employment and wages that can sustain families and purchase individual family housing. While I was doing my primary fieldwork circa 2010, the Japanese lament about "the kids these days" was often more specifically gendered. "Herbivore men" (*sōshoku-*

kei danshi) have been presented in popular media as more interested in girlish things like fashion and baking than more classically masculine activities like climbing the ranks at work and having lots of sex with women. Marketing researcher Megumi Ushikubo, a major writer on the phenomenon, also refers to herbivore men as "ladymen" (*ojō-man*). In her analysis, herbivore men are gender deviants, perversely solitary in their sexual pursuits and unhealthily capable of having platonic friendships with women (2008, 56–70).

However, another major publication that discussed the issue of "herbivore men" around the same time was a self-help guide to romance: *Love-ology for Herbivore Men* (*Sōshoku-kei Danshi no Ren'aigaku*) (Morioka 2008). Its author, Waseda University philosopher Masahiro Morioka—a self-identified herbivore—notes in more academic work that, "[i]n male culture prior to the present, there was a concept that the manly way to do things was precisely to doggedly advance on women, even if they resisted a bit. The idea was that the women might dislike it at first, but that was a mere pose; eventually, they would accept the man. Herbivore men sensitively reject this kind of 'masculinity'" (Morioka 2011). Here, Morioka attempts to recuperate the herbivore man: he isn't queer, he isn't a problem—he's a heroic egalitarian opposed to rape culture.

As for Japanese women, as the discussion of the ohitorisama category above suggests, many women's current understanding of marriage puts it at odds with other goals that they have for their life: a career is something one does for one's self, whereas marriage requires the sacrifice of women's own desires to those of their husbands and children (Nemoto 2008, 226–228). Earlier this century, the way women felt forced to choose between marriage and workforce participation was pinned on the poor work-life balance of Japanese employment structures (Roberts 2005). However, women still seem to be forced to choose one path or another despite the fact that structures of labor have become substantially more flexible in the last thirty years (Mirza 2016). Even if women can *theoretically* combine work and family life, the social pressure to quit working upon marriage—or if not then, upon pregnancy—continues to constrain women's life course options. Aronsson (2015) argues that one force that pushes women out of work is the workplace itself: the feeling that, as women, there's only so much they can do. Through the 1990s into the early 2000s, "although gender ideology and beliefs about the consequences of women working became more egalitarian, beliefs about the importance of work for women became less egalitarian" (Lee, Tufiş, and Alwin 2010, 198). The belief that women need a home and children to be happy—and a home needs a housewife to prosper—have not necessarily become less entrenched in Japan, even as more women work after marriage and childbearing (NIPSSR 2017, 34).

STRAND FOUR: LATE CAPITALISM AND NEOLIBERALISM

Any number of conservative commentators worldwide would like to blame a variety of social ills on the lack of moral fiber they infer from crumbling family structures and falling marriage rates. If only young people would get married, such commentators argue that they would benefit from any number of individual and social goods that marriage is associated with (Coltrane 2001). In the US context, heterosexual, monogamous marriage has been proposed as a solution to poverty and healthcare woes (Bernstein 2006). In Japan, marriage is supposed to bring with it "the joy of normal living" in a middle-class household with a regularly employed (salaryman) husband, a full-time housewife, and children. This ideal has changed little even while such families become more and more rare in practice (Goldstein-Gidoni 2017).

The trouble is, these moralizing commentators have the relationship between marriage and these social goods backwards. It is not that marriage leads to stability and prosperity, rather, it is stability and prosperity that enable people to believe they can marry, or have children. In the United States, research has found that most poor people would prefer to marry, but feel they can't due to precarious finances and housing (Edin and Reed 2005). This would suggest that marriage and childbirth rates have nothing to do with individual moral failure or selfishness, although, especially in Japan, women have been too frequently berated by politicians for the supposedly selfish act of abstaining from marriage and childbearing (Nemoto 2008). Rather, the Japanese situation seems to point to the same conclusion as the American evidence. Many Japanese singles feel keenly that marriage and parenthood are serious obligations, not to be undertaken wantonly, and certainly not without being in an economic or social position to do a good job of it and provide well for their families. Studies of men in low-income, irregular jobs ("freeters") indicate that these men marry at lower rates, in part because they do not feel capable of fulfilling the role of husband and breadwinner—of fulfilling their perceived duties to their families. While Japanese women are increasingly turning toward more companionate ideals of marriage, Japanese men still feel that their earning power—or lack thereof—is a significant barrier to their ability to marry (E. Cook 2014).

We must then ask, if marriage rates are lower around the world, if childbirth rates are lower around the world, what is leading all of these people to feel that they are not really in a position to form families? The straightforward answer is similar economic conditions around the world: the inequality between rich and poor is on the rise everywhere. Japan once characterized itself as "90% middle class," but can now be called a "gap society" (*kakusa shakai*) with growing inequality between regular and non-regular employees, decreasing gains for university graduates, and an inadequate public social safety net that is not able to catch everyone let down by the simultaneous decline of corporate welfare. In addition to the very real social vulnerability that this creates, the feelings of anxiety in a situation of increased precarity also threaten social integration (Hommerich 2012).

This anxiety is felt with a particular depth in Japan, formerly famous for its lifetime employment system. Although many employees, for reasons of class, industry, and particularly gender, were never able to enter into this system, nonetheless, there was a strong belief that a job was a job for *life*, and labor protests in Japan throughout the twentieth century had the effect of minimizing the impact of temporary employment[5] (Gordon 2017). The lifetime employment system was in a sense, peak Fordism: the employee's commitment of labor and loyalty to the company would be rewarded by a living wage that could support a family, a secure position during one's working life, and a secure pension afterwards. In the post-Fordist world, anthropologist Anne Allison (2012) characterizes Japan's young working poor as "ordinary refugees," a paradox that points out both the soul-crushing nature of irregular employment and poverty in Japan, while also emphasizing the truly banal quality of contemporary precarity.

According to Gordon (2017), "non-regular employment" occupied 38 percent of Japanese jobs in 2014, in contrast to "regular employment" on a more-or-less permanent contract. Whether part-time workers, short-term contract workers, or "dispatch" (*haken*) workers hired through a third party, all non-regular employment brings with it decreased access to job training, fewer labor protections, and fewer, if any, guarantees of continued employment or pay raises—despite these jobs offering workers lower pay to begin with. In particular, men employed in non-regular positions are less likely to marry and have children because of their decreased economic circumstances. This "dual employment structure" also has "rigid boundaries" that make it difficult to move from temporary to regular employment, despite the desires of many for more settled work lives (Gordon 2017, 33). This has led to a culture of *shūshoku katsudō*, a twenty-first-century neologism that means, roughly, "job-hunting."[6] Competition for the few remaining jobs with a lifetime employment guarantee is fierce, and for those without a lifetime employment guarantee, job hunting is a fairly constant state of being. This is borne out by Emma Cook's longitudinal work with male and female "freeters," part-time or irregular workers (2016). Many male freeters start looking for a job when they find serious girlfriends, or decide on their own that they want to think about forming families; extraordinarily few find stable work after an entire work history of irregularity testifies against them. And so extraordinarily few marry.

Japanese sociologists, like sociologists around the world, recognize that this is a structural problem, and yet the solution to it—individual effort in job hunting—is profoundly individual, profoundly neoliberal. American anthropologist Ilana Gershon characterizes the distinction between liberal and neoliberal agency as "a move from the liberal vision of people owning themselves as though they were property to a neoliberal vision of people owning themselves as though they were a business" (2011, 539). Relationships thus become "market alliances," and consequently, "neoliberal agency emerges as conscious choices that balance alliances, responsibility, and risk using a means-ends calculus" (540). Each individual thus becomes uniquely responsible for their own success or failure in the world—either the business-self has been managed well and will thrive, or it has been managed poorly and, like any business, will go under.

In Japan specifically, this has manifested as discourse about "self-responsibility" (*jiko-sekinin*). Miyako Inoue describes "jiko-sekinin" as "a key word issuing from recent Japanese developments in which the logic of market fundamentalism has spread into the domains of the social and the individual and thus acts as a moral frame of reference to define the individual's relationship to the society and to herself" (2007, 83). In the context of Japan, particularly, this has meant an evolution *away* from a sense of collective social responsibility and *toward* a sense of individual responsibility for the course of one's life, good or bad. As a result, in Inoue's work on language and gender in the workplace, she found that "interpersonal communication between women and their immediate male supervisors" became interpreted "as the source of, and the solution to, gender discrimination" (2007, 87). A problem with the social structure—entrenched misogyny—gets transposed into the realm of individual behavioral dynamics and as a result, becomes the problem of each individual woman to solve or suffer through, rather than banding together and seeking collective relief.

This, then, is the particular condition of neoliberal Japan (or for that matter, neoliberal Britain, or neoliberal America, or neoliberal anywhere): individual, rather than structural, or collective, responses to social problems have become the norm. Japanese anthropologist Shunsuke Nozawa (2015), writing on the phenomenon of elderly people dying alone and unrecognized (*kodokushi*, "solitary death"), diagnoses the problem as a failure of kinship structures, a lack of interest in collective living, or an inability to do so, brought on by economic conditions. Yet, the solutions proposed by local governments to this problem are individual—for example, neighborhood meet-ups so everyone can get to know each other, or postal services that make sure to hand the mail directly to the recipient at the door, to encourage human interaction and contact.

Similarly, Japan's low rates of marriage and childbirth seem to have clear structural sources, which have long been acknowledged by Japanese sociologists. And now, we come full circle to 2008, when the "marriage-hunting fad" was set off by a popular sociological book called *The Age of "Marriage Hunting"* (Yamada and Shirakawa 2008). The book details a number of changes, particularly to the structure of labor in Japan, that have left Japanese singles without ready places to meet each other, or the economic resources to make marriage happen. And yet, the solution it proposes is, like the others discussed above, ultimately one based on individual effort, in classic neoliberal fashion. *Kekkon katsudō*, or "marriage hunting,"—formed on analogy with *shūshoku katsudō*, "job hunting"—proposes a similar set of activities. In the past—so the story goes—people just fell into job or marriages through everyday social connections. Now, active effort is required to achieve those same outcomes, and the burden of that effort is placed on the individual who wants gainful employment or a spouse.

Structural solutions, like labor laws that decrease employment precarity, increases in wages, or strengthening the social safety net in case of un– or under-employment would make sure that individuals have the resources they need in order to feel that they can marry. But these solutions haven't really been tried. In their absence, many rational, neoliberal, individual actors in Japan have decided that marriage and childbearing are simply too risky. The government, in attempting to address the birthrate, has committed itself to the formation of a "gender-equal society" in a 2005 law. Some observers argue that this law is doomed to failure because it doesn't go far enough. It doesn't go far enough, because it doesn't actually guarantee equality between men and women (e.g., Huen 2007). However, insofar as this law is about giving men and women resources with which to mitigate the risks of marriage and childbearing (by, for example, giving women access to higher-waged jobs), I would argue that its actual problem is that it fails to escape the neoliberal trap of putting the burden on individuals to make good choices. Japan will not overcome its demographic problems until it makes a collective commitment to the welfare of all.

A RESEARCH STORY

In the monograph that follows, I outline the state of both matchmaking and online dating in Japanese society, with a focus on language. The second chapter of this work details the concepts that can help explain the role of language in forging human connection. I focus on "phatic" language, that is, the kinds of language that establish channels of communication between people, from passing conversations to established relationships. This chapter explores some of the history of phaticity as a concept in linguistics and anthropology, and demonstrates the centrality of phatic labor in matchmaking and online dating. It also explains some of the particulars of Japanese linguistic structure that are relevant for understanding how Japanese speakers metapragmatically locate "gender" and "politeness" in specific linguistic forms, and how we can look at the use or avoidance of some forms as a way to understand the kinds of language that are "best" or "most effective" for attracting and appealing to prospective spouses, online and in person.

Chapters 3 and 4 focus on each of my two research "sites" in detail. Chapter 3 focuses on contemporary Japanese matchmaking, from its roots in the nineteenth century to its current, half-online, commercialized manifestations. Based on ethnography and interviews, it lays out how today's matchmakers do their jobs, and their views on the clients they serve and care for. Chapter 4, by contrast, lays out the slightly more chaotic world of online dating. Working off information from ethnography, interviews, and documentary analysis, it discusses the social transformations around online dating in Japan, the attitudes of online daters, and their successes and failures.

Chapter 5 circles back around to the concept of phaticity, discussing the phatic labor of both matchmakers and online daters, and the phatic technology of the internet. It addresses what phaticity can do—and also what it can't. Phatic techniques and technologies like matchmaking and online matching services can expand the pool of potential partners, compensate for busy work lives, and allow individuals to candidly think about what they want from romantic and marital relationships, and then act on those preferences in their search for a partner. But is that enough to make a difference in the face of the forces arrayed against the single people of Japan? This chapter is ultimately about the future, and whether a future based on individual efforts alone can save marriage, save the economy, save Japan.

The stories and sociolinguistic arguments that I present in this monograph, as outlined above, are ultimately the product of a trajectory through time and different community spaces during my preliminary fieldwork in 2007, the main period of research I undertook between April 2009 and March 2011, as well as follow-up research carried out during 2012–2013. My interest in online dating grew directly out of my knowledge about matchmaking, and I have spent my summers between 2015 and 2019 returning to Japan to keep in touch with the state of Japanese matchmaking as well as conduct interviews with friends and acquaintances engaged in online dating as it becomes normalized in Japan.

My interest in matchmaking began with questions of language, gender, and sexuality. Japanese is often held up as a textbook case of distinct gendered speaking styles, with a unique "Japanese women's language." Any Japanese language learner will come across gender-specific prescriptions and prohibitions.[7] As a budding anthropologist in my first few years of graduate school, as I familiarized myself with the literature about this phenomenon, I wanted to know if gendered speech was a component of attractiveness, and more specifically, if linguistic difference was part of heterosexual attraction. Why heterosexual attraction? Much of the research on Japanese women's language defines it relative to men's language, the two gendered speech styles complementing one another. Women's language is polite where men's is rough; cute where men's is blunt; demure where men's is assertive. Janet Shibamoto Smith takes up these issues of language, gender complementarity, and attractiveness by looking at Japanese translations of English-language romance novels, showing how the heterosexual heroes and heroines use stereotypical "masculine" and "feminine" language forms in order to model "where (in language) and how (by being maximally 'feminine' or 'masculine') to locate and enact attractiveness" (2004, 114). My ambitious goal was to see if such linguistic sexual dichotomization played out in real-life conversations between couples—if linguistic masculinity and femininity also helped to constitute each other, and shape attractiveness, off the page.

However, one can easily imagine the difficulties of finding a standpoint from which to approach this question in a practical, anthropological sense, as well as in an ethical sense. But in 2007, I stumbled upon marriage bureaus (*kekkon sōdan-sho*), which held out to me the tantalizing promise of working with matchmakers to see how relationships formed, what kinds of problems their clients encountered, and what was considered attractive in male and female clients, including their language use. That summer, I contacted and visited a small number of marriage bureaus in the Kyoto area, and—with greater and lesser degrees of success—conducted preliminary interviews. A few places granted me second interviews and invited me out for social occasions, after our awkward first meetings. In all cases, these were small marriage bureaus run more or less by one or two people—the kind of businesses that would form the basis for most of my later research.

With my preliminary interviews in hand, along with a stack of brochures and self-help books acquired that summer, I began to reformulate my research questions. Linguistic anthropologists understand gender as something "performed" through repeated, gender-appropriate behavior, such that it comes to seem completely natural (Butler 1990). Now I wanted to know what kind of gender performances led to success finding a partner through a marriage bureau. Would a particular *kind* of masculinity or femininity be more desirable in this context? My view of attractiveness narrowed as I sought to investigate how, in contemporary Japan, a person is judged to be "attractive" *specifically as a marriage partner*, based on both material economic facts as well as semiotic cues to the person's inner character: good dress, a polite and considerate manner, and the ability to skillfully carry on a conversation. I also wanted to know more about the role of the matchmaker in possibly encouraging or coaching clients in their performances of gender. Miyamoto-sensei, the first matchmaker I interviewed at length, heavily emphasized the counseling she provided to her clients. The "sōdan" part of "kekkon sōdan-sho" means "advice," suggesting that the matchmaker's counseling is central to the whole process of learning to perform not just masculinity or femininity, but *marriageability*.

Eventually, funding and research plans in hand, I moved to Japan for what would turn out to be five years in August 2008. Japan had changed in the year or so I'd been away, and it had changed in ways that highlighted precisely the subject of my research. Earlier in the year, popular sociologist Yamada Masahiro had teamed up with a journalist to release a best seller that struck a chord of interpersonal malaise and dissatisfaction in Japan's popular culture. That book, *The Age of Marriage Hunting* (Yamada and Shirakawa 2008), has already been discussed. But konkatsu was now a trend, and advertising for marriage services was (and still is) everywhere I looked (see figure 1.1).

Matchmakers were also beginning to publish their own books promoting their industry. Some published them as advice to the single (Yamada 2008 and 2009); others aimed at curious businesspeople looking to get started in matchmaking (Nakanishi Keiji 2009). In this changed environment, I delved back into research by getting in touch with old acquaintances along with some of the matchmakers I had encountered through blogs and books. My general goal at this point was to understand the evaluative rubrics used by matchmakers when counseling clients. What kind of behavior is desirable in a potential spouse? What is key for making a good first impression? What information do clients look to as signs of someone's inner qualities or real self, in order to determine whether the person they've just been introduced to seems like someone who would make a good marriage partner? How should clients be coached or counseled? How (and in how many different ways) do clients fail during the matchmaking process? Whose responsibility is that failure—the matchmaker's, or the client's?

My initial hope was to build on my interviews by observing a subset of my matchmaker contacts at work directly with clients. Most accounts of participant observation are in some way "sited," which is to say that the anthropologist has a base of operations from which they conduct their research. Around the same time that I was doing my fieldwork, academic friends situated themselves in local hospitals, or centers for adopted

Figure 1.1. A photograph of a blushing bride next to text advertising a partner matching service called O2. They promise to "introduce you to an ideal and appropriate partner" (*anata ni fusawashii risō no o-aite o go-shōkai shimasu*). Photo taken by the author on a train in Tokyo in June 2018.

youth. I aimed to do something similar and find a matchmaker willing to let me use their office as a "site" for my ethnography, in return for which I planned to offer office help, or provide any other business assistance that I could. In addition to observing matchmakers at work, I also hoped to forge ties with clients, so that I could ask them about their experiences with konkatsu more generally and matchmaking more specifically. This interview data was meant to focus on the same topics as interviews with matchmakers, but of course, from the clients' perspective. How did their matchmakers coach them? What difficulties or failures did they encounter? What was the client's rubric for evaluating success or failure, and how was it different from or shaped by that of the matchmaker? And, perhaps most critically: did clients believe that their efforts could succeed, and that they would be able to marry?

As it turned out, about half of my original research plan was feasible. I was indeed able to find a greater number of matchmakers and interview them, meeting with a few for repeat interviews to discuss the finer points of the matchmaking process and clients' behavioral semiotics as I became more and more familiar with matchmakers' practices. I was also, to some extent, able to observe matchmakers at work. However, my ambition to observe matchmakers meeting with and counseling clients turned out to be mostly impractical, because as it turns out, very little of it happens in person. Apart from initial meetings to size up and register new clients, most of a matchmaker's work takes place in confidential emails, texts, or phone calls—I had utterly failed to account for new media. Likewise, I was unable to "site" myself in one office, as I had hoped, since few matchmakers even have them. Most matchmakers use online databases managed by organizations like the NNK, which means that their clients can search for partners from home, their phones—wherever. Matchmakers can likewise work at home or on the go. The few in-person meetings that need to happen can be carried out in convenient cafés, which is also where I wound up doing almost all my interviewing.

This brings me to my next methodological difficulty, which was that interviewing clients turned out to be mostly impossible, with a couple exceptions. Signing up with a marriage bureau can be embarrassing to many clients, or, if not embarrassing, it is at least something that is felt to be quite private. As Kawakami-sensei explained to me, it's embarrassing for prospective clients to come see a matchmaker after hearing about love match after love match. According to another matchmaker, Nakao-sensei, "They come to places like this because they can't find love (*ren'ai dekinai*)." Consequently, few matchmakers seemed willing to put clients in touch with me. I left recruitment fliers with some matchmakers that I was close to, but nothing came of them. Matchmaking is an industry that thrives on trust, and I imagine that sending clients my way would have been a risky move.

Although my access to information about clients' behavior was thus highly circumscribed, this is not to say that the present work is devoid of client voices. I was able to interview a few clients, as well as some individuals pursuing other kinds of konkatsu outside the matchmaking system, for comparative perspectives. Moreover, many matchmakers have turned to the profession in recent years after their own marriages with the help of marriage bureaus. Their narratives of success at matchmaking and subsequent professionalization also form part of the data on clients that I was able to gather during the course of my fieldwork. Getting to the clients' side of the story has also been a motivation for me to look into online dating, which overlaps extensively with matchmaking and other kinds of konkatsu or *koikatsu* ("love hunting"). Many people who use online dating services use them as part of a varied set of strategies, and as a result, some of my online dating interviewees also turned out to have experience with marriage bureaus as well.

However, I also came across some unexpectedly rich sources of information. Through the matchmakers I encountered during the course of my research, I was eventually invited to join the regular meetings of two very different matchmaker organizations. One of these was a small, primarily social, group of matchmakers from Kyoto, Osaka, and Shiga prefectures, who meet more or less bimonthly over lunch to talk shop and share profiles of clients who need a little extra promotion, for one reason or another. The other was a large, national organization of matchmakers which manages a shared, online client database and web infrastructure, and holds regular monthly meetings for their members to clarify policies and address matchmaker concerns: the NNK. They also organize large-scale matchmaking events and offer a variety of training seminars and professionalization opportunities for individuals who want to start their own matchmaking businesses, some of which I was also able to attend. Thus, in participant-observation style, I learned how to be a matchmaker myself: how to pitch my business, develop my own persona as a matchmaker, and establish my authority. I also learned how to advertise and find clients, and what to do with those clients once I had them, that is to say, how to properly counsel them throughout the different steps of the matchmaking process. Even more than my formal interviews and informal chats with matchmakers in various settings, my regular attendance at association meetings and workshops provided me with rich knowledge about how matchmakers learn to do their jobs, how they view their work, how they engage with clients and how they teach each other by example—good and bad.

The organizational and instructional information that I took away from my participation in matchmaker associations, along with my formal interviews with members of the marriage industry, forms the great bulk of my official research data on matchmaking. My lack of access to the client side of the picture in 2009–2011 forced me to both change my focus and reorient my questions. My focus shifted much more exclusively to the matchmakers. In order to properly discuss the communities I participated in and the people I knew, I have to tell you a little bit about who they were, and who they were not, and what matchmaking entailed as a job during the time of my fieldwork.

Yamada Yumiko (2008, 25–45), a published author and successful matchmaker who closely aligns herself with the term nakōdo in her writing, explains in detail the many different kinds of businesses operating under the umbrella term *kekkon sōdan gyōkai* (marriage advice industry). The most visible members of this business are large, national companies such as Nozze (http://www.nozze.com), O-net (https://onet.co.jp/), and Zwei (http://www.zwei.com). Advertisements for these large companies can be readily found—happy brides and grooms proclaim their virtues on trains and subways, so anyone who takes public transport will encounter these services, or similar. When I began my preliminary research in 2007, I knew little about the difference between these large companies and other, smaller businesses. At that time, I made a visit to the Kyoto office of Zwei, located in a posh building in the most downtown location possible, at the corner of Shijō and Karasuma Avenues. They did not know quite what to make of an anthropologist asking for interviews and information, but they did give me a helpful pile of promotional materials. Circa 2009, these large marriage information services were likely the primary businesses benefitting from the konkatsu boom. The information that I cover here is based on promotional materials that I received from different companies, information publicly available on websites, and information learned from interviews.[8]

Generally speaking, marriage information services offer two-year contracts with large up-front fees, in the realm of ¥200,000–¥400,000.[9] This fee purchases clients' online access to the national database of pre-vetted members, and in-person access to the counseling staff at the local branch office of the company. Clients usually set up their own omiai, which makes the experience little different from online dating, except that the marriage information service presumably offers a more rigorously selected and screened set of potential partners who are at least avowedly interested in marriage, and have ready money to put down on this possibility. Considerably less expensive are online companies which offer "net omiai." These are rather like marriage information services, except without the counselors and brick-and-mortar branch offices. Conversely, they are more or less exactly like online dating, except that they have been legitimated via the language of neotraditional matchmaking. Another difference between online dating and net omiai is that the net omiai clients may submit ID documents to prove that, at least, they are who they say they are.[10]

Closer to the individual matchmaker model, there are also *kekkon sōdan-sho*, usually rendered in English as "marriage bureaus." According to Yamada, these are run by individuals, but are affiliated with larger marriage information services and have similar pricing schemes (¥100,000–¥200,000 up front for a two-year contract). As mentioned earlier, sōdan means "advice," and the owners of the marriage bureaus are presumably there to advise their clients about omiai possibilities, and guide them through the process, although according to Yamada, they are liable to take a more hands-off approach than an old-fashioned matchmaker. However, there is a bit of slippage between the marriage bureau and the individual matchmaker, as, in my experience, many individual matchmakers also call their businesses kekkon sōdan-sho. However, in addition to using the word "omiai" to describe what they offer, I found that individual match-makers frequently make use of the "old-fashioned" nakōdo as their job title. This is in contrast to workers at larger partner introduction services, who are instead likely to be styled "marriage counselors" or "marriage advisors" using English loanwords for "counselor" (*kaunserā*) or "advisor" (*adobaizā*).

Having picked out the individual matchmakers—the small-business owners—as the population whose practices I wanted to research, at the same time, my research questions shifted toward ideologies of gender and performance in interaction, rather than descriptions of the performances themselves.[11] In the sections of this monograph that deal with matchmaking, my goal is to present a clear picture of matchmakers' evaluative rubrics, which determine what kind of client behavior is helpful to the cause of marriage, and what is harmful; what contributes to a desirable self-presentation, and what is unappealing; what helps to build a connection with someone, and what gets in the way. I also address how this behavioral calculus may differ for men and women of different circumstances. These evaluative rubrics determine an individual's overall value on the marriage market, with higher values trading for the ability to be choosier about potential partners. Matchmakers often take a distressingly realpolitik approach to marriage—seeking to make it happen for their clients, without necessarily questioning the sexist underpinnings of heterosexual marriage as it continues to be practiced in Japan today. For them, the social and personal pleasures of romantic love and the benefits of extended kin network support make marriage worthwhile, however imperfect.

Finally, matchmakers' evaluative rubrics also determine how any client can raise his or her value, through the interactive, evaluative processes that define selves and social reputations that Nancy Munn called "intersubjective spacetime" (1986, 10–15). "Intersubjective spacetime" is the network created between people in interactions and carried on through individual histories. In Munn's analysis of Trobriand Island society, acts have value insofar as they enable an individual to expand their social worlds over time and space, collecting partners for ritual Kula trade. In a similar fashion, client actions have value insofar as they enable them to expand their own intersubjective spacetimes through connections with other clients, collecting experiences that make them into better dates and partners.

Evaluation is an ideological process, and therefore, this is an account of matchmaker's semiotic ideologies. Specifically, I try to account for how matchmakers determine what behavior could be interpreted as an index. Indices (Peirce 1955) are perceptually available signs that in some sense "point to" something not perceptually available. The classic example is smoke, the sight or smell of which suggests the presence of unseen fire. Some external, observable behaviors are likewise taken to point to someone's internal personal qualities, which cannot be perceived directly. Matchmakers' semiotic ideologies, then, consist of the determination of what behavioral signs point to which personal qualities. But this is a complicated task, because any index can operate within any number of "orders," from sociologically macro to micro-contexts (Silverstein 2003). Consequently, any potentially indexical behavior may not actually point predictably to anything at all. As an example, Ochs (1992) notes that an index may be indirect; use of honorific language may point to "femininity" only through an ideological system linking "femininity," at a second order of indexicality, with "being deferential to others," at the first order. Consequently, it is necessary for matchmakers to regiment and standardize indexical behavior and its possible interpretations—or at least attempt to do so, so that client behavior can be reliably and consistently interpreted as signs of particular inner characteristics like emotional states (love, care), or personality traits (shy, selfish).

Over time, the knowledge that I gained about matchmaking fairly naturally led me to research online dating. In part, this happened as I learned about the client-side experience, thanks to friends who added me to their database free of charge. The clients of matchmakers typically start the process by browsing profiles of other clients online and applying to meet people they like. In the case of matchmaking, the matchmakers will work with clients to set up and actually conduct the meeting. In the case of online dating, users must exchange messages themselves, decide if they want to meet themselves, and organize that first meeting themselves. But the profiles are often similar, especially on domestically-produced websites aimed specifically at konkatsu. Moreover, the internet arm of Japan's partner introduction industry now commonly borrows from the language of konkatsu and matchmaking to situate a new practice within an older one and, in so doing, make it seem safe.

Researching online dating has required me to learn new methods for doing ethnography online, and new theories for understanding what being "online" can mean. Some scholars have moved ethnography entirely online. Tom Boellstorff (2008) starts his ethnography of the virtual world *Second Life* with explicit homages to classic ethnographers Margaret Mead and Bronislaw Malinowski in order to show how the most traditional of ethnographic techniques can translate more or less directly to the study of online communities. By contrast, other scholars deliberately compare offline and online data. Bonnie Nardi's beautifully evocative ethnography of the popular roleplaying game *World of Warcraft* (2009) involved both her own extensive participant-observation as a player combined with in-person interviews with other Warcraft players, and watching the process of play from outside the game. In part, this is because Nardi is to some extent interested in questions particular to games, of how one embodies oneself in an avatar while simultaneously inhabiting an ordinary human body.

My own approach has been inspired by work that examines the online and offline simultaneously, by looking at how people interact with technologies in their lives, how they evaluate these technologies, and how they evaluate the people using these technologies, through formal interviews and through less formal processes of hanging out and storytelling. One example of work that takes this approach is Dominic Boyer's ethnographic study of online journalists in Germany, which draws explicit parallels to the way that both journalists and anthropologists have become "screenworkers," "shifting back and forth between producing texts and managing a variety of information channels" (2013, xi). In so doing, he draws attention to the way that the screen—or increasingly, multiple screens—become vehicles for transmitting information, for evaluating the success of news stories, for reading for work, for pleasure, for news. Boyer does this work not so much by participating in journalism, but through an observation-centered approach that is heavily informed by his own work in a remarkably similar field.

An approach like Boyer's seems increasingly relevant as screens have become pocket-sized. When, truly, can the smartphone owner be said to be definitely "online" or "offline?" Shani Orgad argues that "the offline does not explain the online, nor does the online explain the offline. . . . greater advantage is gained when examining the ways in which each configure the other" (2009, 48). With all this in mind, I started from semi-structured interviews of online daters' experiences, but many of those interviews led to one or both of us getting out our phones, comparing apps, showing off our own profiles, checking out other's profiles, and sometimes being online together. On the whole, I would describe these interviews as joyous. Some of this is because of my changed position in the field, and my changed personal circumstances in life. I started studying matchmaking in my mid-twenties, when I was single; now, I'm in my late thirties and married. Having achieved a kind of "success" at konkatsu, and having past experience of online dating myself, makes me a comrade-in-arms or a coconspirator: I've been there too, and I know what it's like.

Matchmaking comes with documentary treasure troves, but access to them is substantially restricted—one must be a client of a member matchmaker to search any particular organization's database. Online dating, konkatsu, and koikatsu websites, however, are open to anyone who wants to sign up and view them. This presents ethical quandaries for researchers hoping to mine such profiles for data: as is the case with many online spaces, even though the information is publicly available, it has intensely personal qualities to it. Having a profile on a matching site can be a source of tremendous vulnerability for users. Sites themselves take varied approaches to research and data privacy. When I met with representatives from the konkatsu site Zexy Enmusubi in 2015, they encouraged me to make a profile and check the site out for myself. By contrast, the matching app Tinder's "Community Guidelines" explicitly prohibit the creation of profiles for research only.[12] In the aftermath of Wang and Kosinski's infamous (2017) study that claimed it had developed an AI that could distinguish gay and straight faces, based on a cache of images scraped from online dating sites, users themselves are now more aware that their profiles could be put to uses they might never have imagined, and some users on particularly vulnerable apps like LGBTQ+-oriented Grindr may now specify that their profile is not to be used for research.

However—without presenting any particular profile in detail—a qualitative overview of different profiles from different sites and apps is absolutely necessary to an understanding of online dating, and it was in the spirit of gathering this kind of overview data, without archiving revealing information like photographs, that I conducted my initial research on online dating sites, with guidance from my local IRB. Unlike matchmakers, whose practices tend to be more or less the same from organization to organization, each app or site has its own format, its own options for discovering other users, and its own methods for users to signal their interest in each other. Users thus write substantially different profiles across different sites, and reveal and conceal different kinds of information, as well as different *amounts* of information (Alpert 2020). The subject cannot be researched without some experiential understanding of the difference in profile structure and content between international hookup behemoth Tinder, and domestically produced sites designed with specifically Japanese sensibilities in mind.

In addition to the documentary data consisting of the profiles themselves, online partner introduction services also have a wide array of help documentation that can also be used for research purposes. Matchmakers' websites are fairly minimal and repetitive, describing the typical flow of match-making and encouraging clients to sign up from there. The databases they keep are ultimately a tool for a fundamentally human system. When clients need help, they have matchmakers to ask, and matchmakers to mediate communication for them. By contrast, the user of an online dating platform has nothing save the app itself, and any help documentation contained within. Attending meetings of matchmaker associations taught me about consensus and disagreement among matchmakers, and the shifting ideologies they carry into their practices. Apps in and of themselves are relatively static, and their ideologies are revealed through the kinds of information they ask users to supply in profiles along with the kinds of questions they imagine their users asking in help documentation. For example, Dalton and Dales (2016) discuss the help and advertising documentation of five konkatsu sites, arguing that the terms and conditions reinforce the male breadwinner model of family structure, and that differing search suggestions for male and female users reinforce professional labor roles for men and caretaking roles for women (9).

While each app is its own miniature world of gender, marriage, and sexual ideologies, apps dialogue with each other through their very existence: each new platform is developed to fill open niches, or to present users with new, better, or at least more clever systems for helping singles find compatible partners and enabling them to communicate and meet.[13] Thus, in addition to studying user experiences through interviews, and user performances through profiles, it is also possible to study ideologies around online partner matching via the process of reading help documentation and creating a profile. For this, in addition to looking at actual profiles, it is also necessary to look at as many sites as possible, in order to understand, in broad and heterogenous terms, how the world of online partner matching conceptualizes gender, relationships, and society itself.

THE ANTHROPOLOGIST IN AND OUT OF THE FIELD

Ethnographic practices deliberately blur the lines between "work" and "research" and "life." Given that participation in communities is an explicit goal, they are inherently processes of encounter and human interaction. This is to say that my research has been shaped not just by what I did, who I talked to, and what I observed. It was also shaped by who I am—what I look like, my age, gender, race, ethnicity, and language skills—and how matchmakers interpreted my interest in their profession and my presence at their meetings. Likewise, it has been shaped by my friendships, and by online daters' perceptions of me as a friend, acquaintance, or at least, a fellow traveler in the world of dating and marriage. As an anthropologist of Japan, I am required to say something about *nihonjinron*, "theories of the Japanese people," which is a shorthand for the widespread belief held by many ordinary Japanese, as well as policy makers and government officials, that the Japanese people are unique, and wonderful in their uniqueness, but difficult for any outsider to truly understand (Befu 2001 provides an anthropological overview). Yet there is a general pleasure at the sight of young foreigners working hard to learn about traditional, unique, and special Japanese cultural activities and Japanese language studies. An interest in kimono, flower arrangement, Japanese martial arts, or in my case, incense and classical Japanese poetry, is likely to be lauded, praised, and encouraged. Although I did not quite expect this reaction to my study of matchmaking, nonetheless, most matchmakers that I talked to were excited that I wanted to learn about this Japanese tradition as well, and try to share it with an audience overseas.

Additionally, my studies were almost certainly helped along by the fact that, during the time of my main research grant (2009–2011), I was affiliated with one of the most prestigious universities in Japan: Kyoto University. That, and my status as a doctoral student, and later as a professional academic, meant that my research was taken seriously. Matchmakers' eagerness to talk to me may also have something to do with the fact that their profession involves a certain degree of sociability to begin with; they often describe themselves as *sewa-zuki*, that is, enjoying the pleasure derived from taking care of other people. Matchmaking also requires a certain amount of proselytizing in order to convince modern, young(ish) people that they can find happiness through an "arranged" marriage instead of a "love" match. To some extent, explaining the matchmaking system to me must not have been, at first, too different from explaining it to a new potential client, nor must taking care of me have been so very different from the kind of caretaking matchmakers regularly and purposefully engage in.

This was true in spite of ethnic differences that, with *nihonjinron* in mind, one might assume unlikely. Although I'm white, American, and Jewish, at the start of my research I was also in my late twenties, a student, single, and fluent enough in Japanese for almost every conversation. My client-like position can be seen in the kinds of information or experiences that collaborating matchmakers thought would be helpful for me. Kawakami-sensei and Takamiya-sensei, for example, conducted mock introductions over dinner and drinks with me and another male friend/client of theirs who was also present. To some of my collaborators, the most obvious way for me to learn about matchmaking was to participate directly, and in the role to which I was most obviously suited—that is, they wanted to set me up. In many ways, my experience mirrors that of

Japanese-American ethnographer Dorinne Kondo. In *Crafting Selves*, she writes that, "Though my status was in some respect high in an education-conscious Japan, I was still young, female, and a student. I was in a socially recognized relationship of dependency vis-à-vis the people I knew. I was not to be feared and obeyed, but protected and helped" (1990, 15). I believe that I experienced some of the same phenomenon when matchmakers took me on in a client-like way.

On return trips to Japan, especially after I got engaged, I joked with the Nakanishis and other friends that matchmaking had ultimately helped me get married. About two years into my career in Kazakhstan, I found a wonderful historian who specialized in issues of medicine and sexuality. After bonding over our mutual love of Krafft-Ebing's sexological texts and shows on Amazon Prime, we decided to get married in a mere two months. Given that matchmakers generally work with a three-month framework from omiai to engagement, I was right on target! And in truth, moving at that pace would have been unimaginable for me prior to doing my research. But I had been trained to understand, as both matchmaker and client, that if you don't know within three months if you want to marry someone, you don't want to marry them at all.

Over time, however, my contacts' perceptions of me began to change, particularly as I began to participate in matchmaker professionalization activities. When attending meetings with the small, social matchmaker association, it was always understood that I was a student and that I had come there together with my friends. My attendance at the meetings of the larger matchmaker association was much more ambiguous and anonymous; there were enough participants there to just listen and learn that I was not clearly differentiated from them. My regular attendance at meetings and classes led others to perceive me as a fellow matchmaker. And in fact, my presence there was not officially explained by the organization until the last meeting that I was able to regularly attend in August of 2013, when I was introduced and thanked, and invited to say a few words. When questioned about my presence, I always explained that I research matchmaking academically, but it's been suggested to me on quite a few different occasions that I share my knowledge with Americans not by writing a book like this one, but instead by opening up a marriage bureau at home. The NNK matchmaker recruitment website, as of this writing, even includes a tiny picture that shows me together with a group of matchmakers.

Also lurking in the background of my research are my experiences of being young, and single, and socially inhabiting the world of other twenty- and thirty-something singles, with all the attendant pleasures and complaints of that phase of life. As my research has continued, it has also incorporated my own relationships and eventual marriage. Matchmakers have a clear idea of typical problems that Japanese men and women face, and how to fix them. They characterize their male clients as too passive, or often inconsiderate and misogynistic. At the same time, my single female friends were writing songs about precisely the same observation, complaining that Japanese boys are "cute" but "weak" and hoping they might become a little stronger. The situation makes them feel like "zombie grrrlz" relentlessly pursuing "delicious boys"; they fall in love with the ghosts of samurai instead of men here in the present (Nism and Ikeda 2009). My married female friends complained about their marriages—love matches to college sweethearts—which were nonetheless unsatisfactorily passionless. My single friends fell in and out of love, got engaged, canceled weddings. Over time, all of our situations have evolved. My married friends eventually did have children, and some of them divorced. Single friends got married, just as I did, and achieved parenthood themselves.

Much as my own being has affected my research, so too has my research affected my personal life and my friendships. Given my expertise about marriage, dating, and the internet, friends have always felt free, either in groups or privately, to recruit me to share any wisdom I'd gleaned from my research on matchmaking or my knowledge of marriage in Japan in general; to give advice about differences in relationships between North America and Japan; and to give advice about particular relationship problems. More formally, my friends at Kyoto's former Green e Books recruited me to host a friend's gōkon (a kind of informal group date/matching party), and to give a talk on women's sexuality. None of these experiences or stories form part of my research data, except for when friends were also recruited, as per IRB requirements, as research participants. But my experiences with issues of marriage and dating, formal and informal, official and personal, form the background against which I interpret the claims about Japanese men and women made by various players in the marriage industry, or for that matter, claims made by pop-cultural and anthropological literature. The position of the anthropologist is unique in how decidedly local it is; we cannot claim to speak to society-wide trends, but only to show, through our personal experience and informed analysis, how the people we encounter in the course of our research make sense of their lives and actively reiterate and reinterpret the cultural resources and tropes available to them to craft identities and negotiate relationships. Nonetheless, we find patterns.

NOTES

1. https://kekkon21.com/

2. For some commentary on the role of images in matchmaking (and to some extent, also online dating), see Alpert 2019.

3. Specifically, Robertson writes, "[T]he declining birthrate and the rapidly aging population are not really being seriously addressed by the state as political, social, economic, or historical problems . . . but as *biotechnological problems* requiring *biotechnological solutions*" (372, emphasis in original). Consequently, "Roboticists . . . seem to perceive humanoid robots as instruments of nostalgia: as a means to restore, but in an even better and more efficient way, 'the good old days'" (381).

4. Men, of course, do not need a special term to describe happy bachelorhood—but see the discussion of herbivore men.

5. At least, as far as male employees were concerned. Female waged labor outside the home, even today, is still considered secondary to that of men.

6. Literally, "job-getting activities."

7. The extensive literature on gendered language in Japanese is addressed in chapter 2.

8. The Yokohama office of Nozze also answered some questions for me in 2009.

9. In the time I have spent in Japan, yen to dollar exchange rates have ranged from ¥120 to ¥75 per 1 USD, generally settling at a little over ¥100 per dollar. A quick and admittedly inexact mental conversion between currencies can be done by removing two decimal places, for a sense of the scale of the prices. For example, ¥100,000 would be a bit less than 1,000 USD.

10. However, reputable online dating services like the Japanese branch of match.com (http://jp.match.com) offered these same identification services as early as 2008, so this is not exclusive to net omiai, or rather, the overlap between different online options for meeting new people like "net omiai," "net konkatsu," "net koikatsu," and "deai-kei" sites and apps is substantial. This will be taken up in greater detail in chapter 4.

11. This is a stance also taken by Lemon (2000) in her description of ideologies around performances at the Moscow Romani Theater. My experience also resembles Lemon's field experience in its reliance on networks and multisitedness, in that it moves between personal, "at home" connections with matchmakers, and formal, institutional meetings and training sessions.

12. https://www.gotinder.com/community-guidelines

13. My personal favorite is a Tinder clone called "Hater," which matches users based on shared hatreds. https://www.haterdater.com.

2

✛

Crafting Identity
and Dis/Connection
with Phatic Language

Studies of language and gender often take it for granted that speakers will incorporate their genders into their linguistic performances in some way, that gender differences are sufficient to produce language differences. We rarely ask what would happen if different-gendered speakers were somehow encouraged *not* to differentiate themselves. McElhinny's work on how linguistic anthropologists have come to understand and research gender (2003) pushes us to ask when, how, or why it is that gender comes to make a difference in our interactions with others. In order to address this question, we also have to look at when gender doesn't make a difference, even in a situation, like heterosexual matchmaking practices, where gender might seem to be extremely relevant to the proceedings. This chapter examines the question of when and how gender matters in matchmaking and in language more broadly by looking at the art of profile creation and construction in both matchmaking and online dating.

It's facile and boring to say that the internet has transformed global communications, but that's just because it's so completely true. It's also happened so quickly that it's easy to forget sometimes that the internet has a history, and it's also easy to dismiss the influence of older written genres of digital communication. Within my own adolescence and adulthood, I have witnessed the transition from newspaper-based personal ads that I used to browse with my recently divorced mother, to online personal ads. I remember that relatively early online dating sites like Match.com and OKCupid were basically extended personal ads that also had photos.[1] OKCupid, in particular, always seemed to be chastising me for having a profile that was merely 80 percent complete and encouraging me to write more—to take advantage of the relative lack of word limits online. Now, dating app hegemon Tinder eschews the older art of the written profile in favor of snap judgments based on images, with users encouraged to dismiss a profile by swiping left, or express interest by swiping right, before reading anything at all. In fact, the app is designed so that it takes more gestures—more work—to read through a profile than to swipe quickly past it. Culture writer and researcher Anne Helen Petersen (2014) has argued that the fast-paced semiotic judgments encouraged by Tinder's swiping system lead users to swipe along largely classist and racist lines.

Even so, language plays a prominent role in how we display ourselves and reach out to each other through the evolving genre of the profile. Even Tinder makes space for various kinds of verbal appeals to the reader, and all matching sites and apps make use of writing in profiles, status messages, and at a minimum, direct messaging within the website. My interviews with online daters in Japan suggest that even on Tinder, users who don't write anything in their profiles are at a disadvantage, and writing the "correct" kind of profile on any site strongly affects whether the viewer will respond positively or negatively. Japanese Tinder users don't seem to be alone. Research on Tinder users in Oslo, Norway, suggests that profile text and other information is a functional bonus that has the power to more strongly engage users, especially women (Rocha 2018, 72). Ward (2016) discusses the way that Dutch Tinder users play with their profiles, updating them to see how people will react and achieve different effects, which can include adding or deleting profile text, or uploading images of text in lieu of a more typical profile picture. Her respondents clearly made the effort to read profile text, in spite of the app design that discourages it. Regardless of which app it appears on, the matching site profile is a balancing act that must say something useful about its subject while also being neither too clichéd, nor too weird, nor too off-puttingly suggestive of sexual desire alone. And, while we might not think of neotraditional matchmaking as a kind of "online dating," nevertheless, profile creation and viewing happens primarily online, and matchmakers put significant effort into the art of editing clients' profiles so that they properly show them off to their best advantage, as well as teaching new matchmakers this art. Many of the same linguistic constraints and potentialities inhere in both kinds of profiles, especially when matchmakers' profiles are compared to the kinds of profiles put together by users of matrimonial (konkatsu) sites.

In order to understand how this profile balancing act is accomplished by matchmakers and internet users in Japan, we first need to understand some broader linguistic principles, as well as some particularities of Japanese grammar and usage. This chapter has three goals. First, it introduces linguistic anthropological approaches to language and gender more broadly, and also addresses how those issues manifest in Japan more specifically. Second, it discusses the concept of "phaticity" in greater depth as a way to understand why konkatsu seems necessary in contemporary Japan, along with why matchmakers and clients are tasked with particular kinds of verbal labor. Both matchmaking and online dating are systems where professional phatic laborers (matchmakers and site designers) assist laypersons in establishing new communicative channels, with the hope that these channels will develop into durable pathways, and their clients will develop a durable relationship. Much of this labor involves a kind of active empathy and perspective-taking that encourages men to adopt speech habits associated with femininity, while simultaneously encouraging women toward more self-assertive, "masculine" speech habits. Finally, it suggests that centering phaticity and connection leads to more polite speech within matchmaking encounters, and to particular kinds of profile writing in Japanese in both matchmaking and online dating contexts. This may have the effect of de-emphasizing highly gendered speech patterns that characterize Japanese language ideologies, media, and education, in favor of a kind of linguistic androgyny where it becomes impossible to guess the gender of a profile author.

GENDERING THE SELF IN JAPANESE

Speakers of Indo-European languages are accustomed to having some options in second-person forms of address, to express concepts like "intimacy" or "solidarity" through a "familiar" second-person pronoun, and "distance," "respect," or "hierarchy" through a "formal" second-person pronoun. By contrast, the array of pronouns available to speakers of Japanese, along with verb forms and special honorific vocabulary, can be dizzying to the uninitiated. While Japanese pronouns and honorifics can signify multiple meanings like those above, they can also suggest differences in age, social class, and regional origin and dialect. But one overarching way that students of Japanese and sociolinguistics are often taught to make sense of this diversity is by viewing it through the lens of gender. They learn that men and women in Japan speak in predictably different ways, using different pronouns for first- and second-person reference, and that they vary in their use of other grammatical forms, such as honorifics and sentence-final particles. (These latter may be very briefly characterized as verbal punctuation that expresses the speaker's emotions about what they have just said: doubt, surprise, emphasis.) This is evident from textbooks, which, for example, hold up Japanese to the introductory

sociolinguistics student as a paradigmatic example of gender differentiation in speech and language ideology via its supposed possession of a
"Women's Language," alongside gender differentiation in several Native
American and South African languages (see, for example, Mesthrie et al.
2009, 215–216). Moreover, example conversations in textbooks of Japanese for second-language learners depict textbook characters using "feminine" sentence final particles more often and regularly than can be found
in natural talk (Kawasaki and McDougall 2003), reinforcing for learners
that these feminine-coded forms are used mainly by feminine speakers.

The belief that men and women speak differently is also consistently
reproduced across Japanese fictional works. Shibamoto Smith (2004)
found that Japanese translations of English-language romance novels
consistently translated the dialogue of male and female characters with
stereotypical gendered forms that could not possibly be part of the
original English. This is unsurprising since, from the historical inception
of gendered speech in Japanese, it was associated with fictional female
speech. Inoue's work describes the creation of women's language as a
register via the literary practices of novelists in industrializing nineteenth-
century Japan (2006). Male authors who wanted to bring Western-style re-
alism to Japanese literature used the overheard speech of "schoolgirls" to
craft a literary voice for women in their novels. Eventually, this feminine
voice filtered through to less literary genres (domestic novels, women's
magazines) and was eventually—to some extent—adopted by women
themselves as they echoed the language that had become emblematic of
women's modernity in writing. This back and forth movement between
art and life continues to give the ideological construct of "Japanese Wom-
en's Language" a vibrant social life and sense of verisimilitude to real
women's speech, despite the fact that it has always been more stereotype
than reality.

What, we might ask, does "Japanese Women's Language" consist of?
At its most general, Japanese women's language consists of language that
is self-effacing and deferential to others, although it is important to note
that the "schoolgirl speech" that forms the historical basis of contemporary women's language was originally considered vulgar (Inoue 2002,
406–408). Robin Lakoff (1973), in her groundbreaking work on "Language
and Women's Place," suggested that American women, on the whole, are
more likely to speak in a polite and uncertain fashion, on account of the
generally lower position they occupy in society, relative to men. Cross-
linguistically, Lakoff's assertions about "women's language" don't hold
up, because they depend on a particular cultural image of women as not
just inferior to men, but also as delicate, refined creatures, given to great
emotional sensitivity and also fragility. Elsewhere, even where women
are systematically regarded as inferior to men, they may nonetheless also

be perceived as overflowing with emotion, such that they cannot help outbursts of rudeness or profanity (e.g., Keenan 1989, Kulick 1993). Linguistic strategies that emphasize politeness and high sensitivity to others' feelings, as Penelope Brown (1998) notes, may also be deliberate strategies in the context of systematic violence against women, rather than being an expression of a sensitive and feminine inner nature. However, gender stereotypes in Japan are similar to the American stereotypes identified by Lakoff, as Ide Sachiko notes in her response to Lakoff's work (2004), and have a similar regimenting effect on ideas about what kinds of language are appropriate for women: polite, refined, and hesitant.

As a matter of Japanese grammar, "Japanese Women's Language" tends to manifest in three domains: pronouns, sentence-final particles, and honorific usage. As mentioned above, many speakers of European languages will be familiar with a contrast between a "formal" and "informal" second-person pronoun, such as thou/you in Middle or Early Modern English, tu/vous in French, tu/usted in contemporary Spanish, or ty/vy in Russian. Japanese expands this distinction in the second person into many more different levels: honored you (*anata*), you my darling (*anata, kimi*), you bastard you (*temē*), among others. This distinction also exists in the first person, with more humble first person pronouns that efface the self and show deference to others (*watakushi, watashi*), cute and friendly first-person pronouns (*uchi, boku*), avuncular and rustic first-person pronouns (*washi*), and self-aggrandizing pronouns too (*ore*). Although these pronouns index a number of different possible speaker identities, and it is not entirely possible to lay them out two-dimensionally on a line from "self-effacing" to "self-asserting," or from "masculine to feminine," nonetheless figure 2.1 makes an attempt.

As can be seen from this graph, the more formal, self-effacing, humble pronoun options are typically associated with feminine speakers, while the more aggressive and boisterous pronoun options are typically the province of male speakers—at least ideologically.

Sentence-final particles work similarly. As the name suggests, these "particles" are small, frequently one-syllable units that appear at the end of an utterance in Japanese. They are used to transform statements into questions of various kinds, or emotive exclamations. That is, they express affective content, like doubt or excitement, about the semantic content of the sentence they follow. Sentence-final particles expressing different degrees of excitement or emphasis could be arranged much like the pronouns above, with the delicate *wa* on the feminine end of the scale, and the extremely emphatic *ze* on the masculine end.

In addition to these emphatic particles, tag question markers like *ne* ("isn't it") or *kashira* ("I wonder"), especially the latter, tend to be associated with feminine speech, as they index a stance of delicate uncertainty.[2]

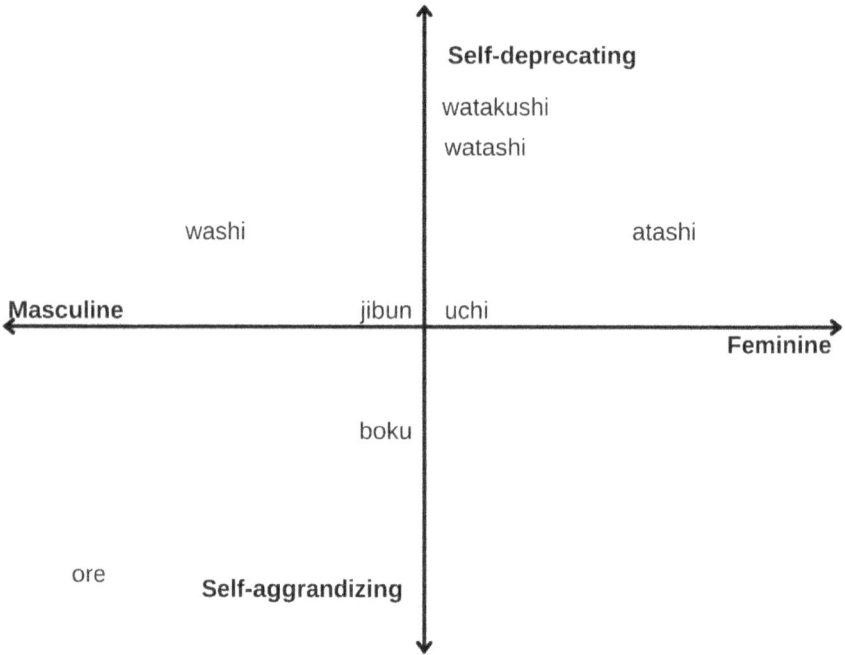

Figure 2.1.   Japanese first-person pronouns, arranged on a gendered axis (horizontal), and a politeness or self-assertiveness axis (vertical). Japanese pronouns that are self-deprecating tend to be "feminine," and conversely, extremely self-aggrandizing or self-assertive pronouns tend to be "masculine," but these relationships are only approximate. Created by Author.

Masculine tag questions are possible, but they are more paradigmatically formed with *na* or *ka na* at the end of a sentence, sometimes with an elongated vowel.

Finally, there is the matter of honorifics. Japanese generally possesses two types: addressee honorifics and referent honorifics. The first are called *teineigo* in Japanese linguistic traditions: "polite language." They consist primarily of the *-masu* suffix on verbs, which signals something much more like the meaning of a "formal" or "polite" second-person pronoun in Indo-European languages. The plain form of any verb, like *taberu* ("eat"), is reserved for conversation with intimates. The suffixed form *tabemasu* means precisely the same thing ("eat"), but shows social distance between speaker and addressee, and expresses a deferential stance.

The second type of honorifics are referent honorifics, that is, they show social distance between the addressee and the person being referenced or discussed in the third person, and are typically called *keigo* (honorific language) in Japanese sociolinguistics. These come in a variety of forms:

Weak Emphasis

wa

Masculine   yo
                                              Feminine

zo

ze   Strong Emphasis

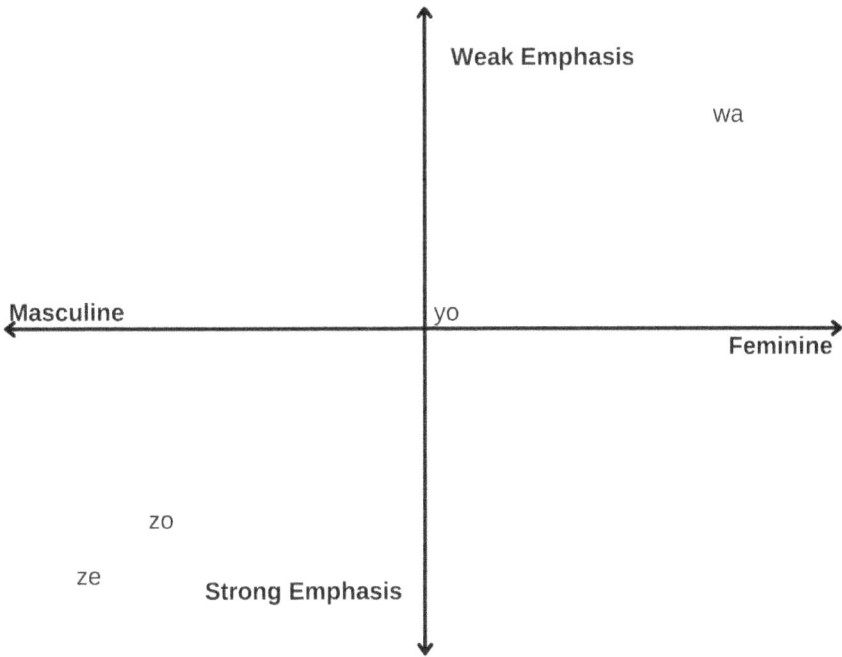

Figure 2.2.   Some common sentence-final particles in Japanese, arranged similarly to figure 2.1. Here, the relationship between gender and self-assertive, or highly emphatic speaking is more straightforward. To get a sense of how strong or even vulgar it is to end a sentence with ze, note that both zo and ze are used to translate the emphatic sense of "fucking" in English. Created by Author.

would-be titles that follow names, such as *-san* or, the more honorific *-sama*, or the more specific *-sensei* for teachers and other professionals. Honored persons' actions may be described with special honorific verbs. *Taberu* describes the act of an ordinary person eating; the honored person's consumption would be described with *meshiagaru*. Where special honorific vocabulary does not exist, ordinary verbs can be transformed into keigo verbs following the formula *o*-verb stem *ni naru*. So, for example, we can take the ordinary *kau* ("purchase") and derive the honorific form *o-kai ni naru*. Conversely, one's own actions may be described with a special set of self-effacing verbs, to further increase the social distance between speaker and referent. These constitute a subset of keigo called *kenjōgo*, or "humble language." Finally, nouns connected to honored persons may also be made honorific through the addition of the prefix *o* or *go*, or through special vocabulary, or both. Thus, my own parents are simply my *ryōshin*, but the parents of someone else that I am speaking to, whom I surely would wish to honor, are conventionally their *go-ryōshin*.

My own house is an ordinary *ie*, but another's house may be an *o-taku* or an *o-uchi*. Some nouns are virtually always honorific, as a perpetual social nicety: *o-kane* (money), or *o-cha* (tea).

Given that language forms are always multifunctional, the various pragmatic uses to which honorifics are actually put are varied, and can range from deference to others (their purported use), to deference to third parties not actually present (H. Cook 2011, 3666–3667), institutional belonging (H. Cook 2011, 3663–3666; 3667–3670), and political maneuvering and insult (Shibamoto Smith 2011), among others. None of these honorific forms are particularly associated in any essential way with feminine speech. Rather, the expectation is that women will use both polite language and honorific language more regularly, more extensively, and more elaborately than men will. That is, women are expected to use honorifics of various kinds as a matter of course, being generally polite to everyone. Men will use honorifics as circumstances demand, with a sense that they are not required nearly as often. Men's conventionally accepted range of expression is generally greater, with access to both the most polite and the most rude expressions available to Japanese speakers. Women's range, by contrast, is artificially skewed toward polite speech.

While "men's" and "women's language" are firmly entrenched in fiction, research in sociocultural linguistics over the last twenty or so years has shown clearly that gender is only one aspect of the sociocultural context that influences the linguistic choices that speakers make, and the forms that they use. For example, hierarchies at work are often relevant. Whether one is speaking to friends or one's boss—whether one is oneself a boss or an underling—all affect the choices of pronouns, politeness forms, and other linguistic variables that are typically associated with gender. Men might therefore speak in "feminine" ways, and women in "masculine" ways, where the context is appropriate. SturtzSreetharan (2006a), in some of the only work dedicated to looking specifically at the language of Japanese *men*, discusses "gentlemanly gender," that is, men's use of "polite" forms more associated with women even in "casual conversation." This is not effeminate, in context, but rather, part of how men present themselves through their linguistic choices as white-collar professionals, using language that is "relatively polite . . . correct, and above all (gender) neutral" (88).

This example demonstrates two things. First, gender is multiple—not just cross-culturally, but intra-culturally. We may speak of "hegemonic masculinity," that is, "the configuration of gender practice which guarantees (or is taken to guarantee) the dominant position of men and the subordination of women" (Connell 2005, 77). Hegemonic masculinity is thus one kind of masculinity in relation to other kinds of masculinities and femininities, arranged in a rough but intersectional hierarchy with factors such as race, class, and sexuality. Different masculinities and the hierarchical relationships between them are constructed through inter-action, for example, American fraternity members jockeying for social position are actively negotiating whose masculinity is literally on top (Kiesling 2001). Femininity is likewise plural, and some femininities are more positively evaluated than others under the regime of hegemonic masculinity. The linguistic literature on Japan is full of "naughty teenage girls" who resist the enforced politesse of Japanese Women's Language through erotically charged slang (L. Miller 2004), much of which is now mainstream. Likewise, it is also full of young women eager to reclaim some of the power they see in men's speech for themselves who, conse-quently, appropriate more assertive "masculine" speech forms as part of a less retiring language style that matches a more ambitious femininity (Okamoto 1995).

Sexual and gender minority communities are also places where hege-monic gender signifiers are melted down and reshaped to serve queer masculinities and femininities. Hideko Abe (2010, 42–46), for example, discusses the use of "masculine" language forms in the 1990s Tokyo les-bian community. While she observed contextual variation in first-person pronoun usage, she also noted overwhelming preference for the low-key masculine *jibun* (literally, "self") by both younger lesbians and gender non-conforming *o-nabe*. Lunsing and Maree (2004), in looking at the speech of gay men and lesbians, note how their speech varies contextually in order to at times challenge, at times uphold heterosexist and hegemonic ideas about masculinity and femininity. Examples include the shift from the subversively feminine "watashi" to more neutral/masculine "boku" as a pronoun for gay male activists; *onē-kotoba*, or "older sister speech" that combines typically "feminine" pronouns and sentence-final particles with vulgar content and lexical items in camp speech; and lesbians who may feel compelled to use feminine "watashi" for themselves or, in one poi-gnant example, resist pronouns altogether and use only their names when specific self-reference is discursively required. It is impossible, therefore, to draw a straight line between "self-expression" or "identity" in language and the immediate and constantly shifting context in which that language is used. Identity and self-expression are always negotiated in and through language, in real time, moment to moment, in particular contexts.

The second point, which is perhaps the more important one, is that gen-der is not always the most relevant thing about a person. Signaling one's professional status or place in a corporate hierarchy may take precedence over signaling masculinity or femininity through strongly gendered lan-guage. This is borne out by studies of professional women in Japan and elsewhere. Kitzinger (2007) argues that even when people signal their gender in talk through such means as describing themselves as "women," that doesn't mean that gender is central to the interaction at hand. In an analysis of a call to a birth crisis line, which helps women struggling with the experiences of new maternity, she shows how the operator constructs herself as authoritative and experienced through reference to the women she's helped professionally, and how the caller constructs herself as heroic, strong, and capable through a narrative of a challenging birth experience leading to lingering anxiety. In neither instance is gender central.

In fiction, using gendered language can be a central component of negotiating attractive, heterosexual Japanese femininity and life as a romance heroine (Shibamoto Smith and Occhi 2009), but this is a poor mirror of actual linguistic practice. Much of the online and offline matching practices discussed herein are heterosexual, marriage is (for the moment) an exclusively heterosexual domain in Japan, and it is the license to search for a spouse that makes many of the practices discussed here socially acceptable. But this is a *specific kind* of heterosexuality that emerges in the *specific institutional contexts* of matchmaking, online dating, and Japan's shrinking population. In the heterosexuality that exists within this space, gender differentiation in language—to the extent that it exists at all in actual Japanese speech practices—is in fact subsumed by politeness and a need to take the perspective of one's conversation partner. Russian theorist Mikhail Bakhtin describes "active understanding" of languages as occurring when "[t]he speaker strives to get a reading on his own word, and on his own conceptual system that determines this word, within the alien conceptual system of the understanding receiver" (1981, 282). And this is what single men and women need to do—imagine the mental terrain and emotional needs of the "opposite" sex, and adjust their language with this in mind. It is a heterosexuality based on *approach* to the other, rather than *distinction* from the other.

Thus, in addition to the well-documented existence of different masculinities and femininities, and the questioning of the relevance of gender within most interactions, numerous studies within linguistics and anthropology have been devoted to transgender or third-gender performances around the world that transgress different cultural expectations for how bodies align with the signs of "man" or "woman" across multiple semiotic domains (see, for example, Newton 1979; Gaudio 1997; Hall 1997; Kulick 1998; Robertson 1998; Barrett 1999; and much more recently, Zimman 2017). A specifically trans linguistics is a growing area of research and theory. One thing, however, that has rarely been addressed as a gendered stance in and of itself is *androgyny*. I use the word "androgyny" deliberately because it seems to me that the matchmakers I worked with absolutely encouraged men to incorporate "feminine" attitudes to communication and conversation into their repertoires. Rather than encouraging their clients to be stoic and silent manly men, matchmakers suggest that their male clients would do better with women by approximating and accommodating "feminine" conversational features. Although the situation might seem radically different, it is actually quite similar to what McElhinny (1995) described as the "cool bureaucrat" masculinity of 1990s police officers. "Cool bureaucrat" was a new model of masculinity in policing that existed in tension with, and in opposition to, a more physically aggressive and hegemonically masculine style that McElhinny called the "crime control" model. To be a "cool bureaucrat" is to be a less literally aggressive masculine figure.

While male clients are encouraged to be more feminine in their communicative habits, female clients in the care of Japanese matchmakers are encouraged to be romantically and verbally assertive, actively looking to meet men and engage with them, instead of passively waiting for men to make all the moves. If they have doubts, they are encouraged to voice them, along with their feelings. Alexy's work on divorce in elderly Japanese couples in neoliberal Japan (2011) notes that relationship models are changing even for this demographic. While older models of Japanese marital intimacy were based on instrumental demonstrations of affection and interdependence between partners, the new paradigm is based on verbal demonstrations of affection and individual self-assertion of needs in relationships, a worldview that lines up with matchmakers' ideas about the ideal way for clients to communicate so that a relationship can move forward *toward* marriage.

Little about the extant sociolinguistic literature on Japan or anywhere else encourages a consideration of androgyny, although there are a few things here and there: a discussion of speakers' perceived genders in Britain (Giles and Marsh 1979). A paper finding absence of gendered language use in the "About Me" section of MySpace profiles (Fullwood, Morris, and Evans 2011). A little more recently, scholarship exploring the emergence of distinctly non-binary speech styles in English, as its own kind of gendered phenomenon (Gratton 2016). In Japanese, Ryan Redmond (2015) explored manifestations of typical men's language in boys' love manga. In this genre, while both main characters are men, they have fixed, stereotypical, and perhaps differently-gendered positions as *seme* (top) and *uke* (bottom). While such manga are often perceived as androgynous spaces of gender play (especially because they are regarded as women's literature), in fact, both seme and uke use rather typical masculine language. Miyazaki Ayumi (2016), in exploring the first-person reference patterns of Japanese middle-school students, finds a certain degree of androgyny appearing, to the extent that stereotypically feminine first-person pronouns are avoided by all speakers, and girls' use of "masculine" first-person pronouns has become mostly normalized. So, there is some research: just not much.

Most of the substantial literature on language and gender in Japan, much of it written in Japanese or by Japanese authors, documents actual differences between men's and women's speech patterns in life and in fiction. However, much of it is also deeply concerned with the metapragmatic salience of gendered language, that is, the extent to which it is explicitly discussed as a social phenomenon and used to both describe and *discipline* the way men and women speak. Such discipline often happens in the context of advice books—a prominent genre in Japan (Bardsley and Miller 2011), or in other literature aimed at women, such as magazines.

Inoue (2004) documents two historical crises around the development of "women's language" as an ideology. The first was at the turn of the nineteenth century, when the vulgar speech of "schoolgirls"—the elite young women who could afford to attend newly opened secondary schools for female students—"pained the ears." Magazine commentators on language exorcised their anxieties around modernization by theorizing the origins of schoolgirl speech in the class confusion that followed the reestablishment of the monarchy and the reestablishment of Japan's feudal caste system. Approximately one hundred years later, in the 1980s and 1990s, "women's language" had firmly been established as a category of language. Women also entered the workplace in greater and greater numbers—again, creating feelings of anxiety around gender and class. Letters published in newspapers bemoaned women's apparently degraded linguistic abilities, with masculine features in their speech and sub-par honorific vocabularies. All of this literature served to shame and hopefully discipline women for departing from previously established norms of gendered speaking—whatever those norms might have been.

One of the founders of modern linguistics, Ferdinand de Saussure, famously divided language into *langue* and *parole*, or, in English, "language" and "speech." *Langue* refers to systems and norms of language that apply to whole populations of speakers, while *parole* refers to what people actually say (Saussure 1959, 13–14). I originally began to consider the issue of androgyny when trying to solve one of the bigger mysteries of my fieldwork: the near-complete absence of talk about gendered language in matchmakers' accounts of their clients' behavior and failings. What seemed to be relevant at the level of belief about language, in grammars and textbooks and linguistic studies, seemed to be completely absent in matchmakers' own metapragmatic discussions of what their clients needed to know in order to communicate with partners during omiai and afterwards. This was especially remarkable given that so much of what clients seemed to fail at was precisely talking to each other. However, it was also very clear that matchmakers' encouragement of androgyny is limited to linguistic androgyny. The possibilities for linguistic androgyny may hinge on the emphasis of gender divides elsewhere in partner-introduction practices. As Dalton and Dales (2016) note, much of the existing literature on "marriage hunting" in Japan emphasizes, or is predicated upon, a traditionally gendered division of household labor where men work outside the home and women, inside. Matchmakers, like other commercial actors in the "marriage hunting" world, have similar biases about the appropriate contributions of men and women to the household. As just one example, men's profiles *must* list their income. By contrast, women's profiles *never* do even when—perhaps especially when—the woman's income is substantial. Perhaps it is precisely because the role of gender in the process and conduct of marriage is so *obvious* and *entrenched*, it becomes possible to encourage more androgynous norms of interaction, insofar as clients are asked to acquire traits associated with the "opposite" sex in order to appeal to them.

This is most obviously the case with regard to conversational norms, rather than the specific linguistic forms such as pronouns or sentence-final particles discussed above. Women's understandings about the function of conversation in intimate relationships are privileged, and explicitly taught to men by matchmakers (see also Alpert 2014). In many other instances, matchmakers simply do not assign a gender to the personal qualities that are conducive to marriage, and encourage men and women alike to adopt them. The matchmakers that I interviewed do not often distinguish between what men should do or women should do; rather, they tend to talk about what *people* should do, and thus set up gender-neutral standards for appealing behavior. My interviewees typically use gender-neutral terms when describing their clients, like *kaiin* (client), *hito* (person), or *ko* (literally "child" and often specifically "girl," but in context can refer to men as well). Note, for example, the language used by Ishiguchi-sensei (himself a male matchmaker):

何人目に結婚できるかとか、あるいはなん、あのう、何年でやったら結婚できるかというのは、不明。わっかんない。ま、だけど見ていたらその人柄ね？その人が、素直でこっちの言ったことちゃんと聞いてくれる人が早い。

It's not clear that they [clients] can marry after they meet, however, many people, um, that after however many years, doing this, they can get married. You don't know. But, well, if you look at it, their personality, right? Those people, people who sincerely and properly listen to what I say, are faster.

In the original, as is typical of Japanese discourse, the subject is elided, which I have freely translated with third- and second-person pronouns where appropriate. When referred to directly, however, clients are simply people (*hito*, 人). In the realm of interpersonal interaction, differences between genders may actually be erased, suppressed, or minimized within the framework of matchmaking.

GENDER AND PHATICITY

The section above takes it for granted that language is multifunctional. The wealth of Japanese pronouns show clearly that the same forms that convey semantic meaning like "I" or "you" simultaneously convey meaning about who the speaker is in terms of their social position—or at least, who they imagine themselves to be, or who they might want the listener to believe that they are, or how the relationship between them stands. The various functions of language are thus seamlessly laminated atop each other, so that any utterance conveys information about the world at the same time that it does practical social work like managing identities and relationships. However, before language can even begin to do any of this, speakers must establish a working connection between them that allows the rest of the conversation to proceed. Language that fulfills this function—*phatic language*—includes greetings and goodbyes that open and close the channel of communication. It also includes clarifying utterances like "I can't hear you," or the repeated cries of "Are you there? Can you hear me?" that have always been common to long-distance real-time communication as a result of dodgy phone lines, cellular signal, or internet connections. Such expressions check the stability of the channel, and seek to maintain or repair it so that communication can continue.

The definition of phatic language above derives primarily from the one developed by Roman Jakobson (1990). For Jakobson, phaticity is one of a delimited list of six language functions that correspond to six elements of interaction. For example, where the "referential" function of language corresponds to the need to "reference" the surrounding context, the "phatic" function of language pertains to what Jakobson called the "channel" of communication, and served to open, close, and sustain this channel. However, Charles Zuckerman, in his work on what he calls "phatic violence," reminds us that the concept of phaticity was first introduced by Bronislaw Malinowski in 1923 as part of the expression "phatic communion." By "phatic communion," Malinowski meant that simply talking to another person, opening a channel of communication, seems to simultaneously create a kind of human connection, a bond of positive fellow-feeling. These definitions are difficult to reconcile. For Jakobson, contact *per se* does nothing: it's simply a precondition for further linguistic contact. By contrast, for Malinowski, contact itself is the foundation of social relations, or at least, for solving "the problem of meaning in primitive language."[3]

Despite the incommensurability of these definitions, however, much work on phaticity seems to take for granted that contact is in and of itself good, or at least, seems to describe folk theories of phaticity that assume its inherent goodness. For example, Julia Elyachar's work on "phatic labor" (2010) argues that regular relationship maintenance through seemingly "meaningless" chat among the women of Cairo sets up an infrastructure of relationships through which various social goods can be transmitted. Zuckerman (2016), in trying to forward a theory of "phatic violence" as opposed to "phatic communion," objects to what he sees as Elyachar's conflation of phatic labor with positive social results. As he demonstrates by looking at insults and distractions in gambling and sports, linguistic (and interpersonal) contact can just as often be antisocial, violent, and un-wanted. Therefore, we have to disentangle contact as a technical linguistic phenomenon from its emotional or social results, which are varied and unpredictable. In a similar vein, Erving Goffman observed that the simple fact of interacting with other humans makes us physically and mentally vulnerable to each other. Face-to-face interaction inherently contains within it the possibility for violence, dominance, and hierarchy as much as it contains the possibility for approach and intimacy (1982, 4). But for Goffman, and for the matchmakers that I worked with, the risk must be taken, for while communion does not *automatically* proceed from contact, it is nonetheless impossible without it. This justifies, for example, risky strategies like using dramatically edited profile pictures as a means to get clients to meet each other, to bring them into contact with each other, even at the risk of clients feeling disappointed in, or defrauded by, their part-ners (Alpert 2019). A conversation is the precondition for a relationship, marital or otherwise, and phatic language is the prelude to conversation.

In addition to viewing phatic language as a precondition for other kinds of talk, as suggested by Elyachar (2010), we can also view communicative channels as something more like a communications infrastructure than a single phone call—not limited to a single interaction. We can liken it to building cellular towers or laying down cables to transmit signals. Even if sometimes the network is silent, such infrastructures are more or less per-manent installations connecting various points: mobile phones, houses, computers, and the people who use them. Like a cellular network, this infrastructure must be built, and infrastructure can also decay, fall apart, or be purposefully deconstructed. But unlike a single message that travels through the network, infrastructure *persists*, and requires regular use and maintenance—phatic labor—in order to remain open and useable. As mentioned above, Elyachar's work documents the practices of women in Cairo who cross town to routinely visit each other, chat, and gossip—lin-guistic activities that are often dismissed as being uninformative and not especially valuable. But this view is tremendously short-sighted. Regular conversation keeps channels of communication open. Moreover, these channels of communication can become conduits through which various kinds of value can flow, such as economic opportunities, goods, and services. Without necessarily viewing phatic labor as a kind of positive phatic communion, we can still appreciate that Elyachar's work provides us with a wonderful description of exactly how "networking," as we might call it, builds lasting relationships and transforms social capital into the ordinary, material kind.

At the same time—in addition to the critiques levied by Zuckerman—Elyachar's work is open to a potentially neoliberal interpretation. We have seen that social structural problems in Japan have been met with calls for individuals to solve them through individual activity, following the neoliberal paradigm of "self-responsibility." But it is not just that individuals are being called upon to act. They are being called to a specific *kind* of action: phatic labor. The hope is that it will create the kinds of relationships and communicative channels that can serve as durable conduits for material aid—that phatic labor will repair a social infrastructure that many Japanese see as having fallen into disrepair. In Nozawa's study of "solitary death" (2015), we find that elderly Japanese are at risk of dying alone because various kinds of social bonds (*en*), from the family to the workplace, are no longer interesting or compelling to people. Individuals must therefore be pushed to form *new* bonds through phatic labor. Children are tasked with writing letters to the elderly, and mail carriers no longer deliver to a mailbox, but literally make contact by bringing post to the house and physically handing it to recipients (383).

In a similar vein, *shūkatsu*, "job hunting," resembles the omnipresent need to "network" found in Anglophone job hunting advice, for without a reliable infrastructure of "contacts" who can pass on employment opportunities or vouch for job candidates, there is no path through which capital or opportunities can move. The injunction to perform konkatsu in Japan, which started as a trend and seems to have become a routine expectation, can be seen as a similar demand for singles to engage in phatic labor—to reach out and contact others, or at least, make themselves available to be contacted, through activities like attending singles' parties, signing up with matchmakers, or creating profiles using online dating services. A profile in a matchmaker's database or on a matching app can be understood as another piece of phatic infrastructure: an open point of contact, which can be utilized by anyone who comes across it to send a like (*iine*).

Within this paradigm of phatic labor, we can understand Japanese matchmakers as phatic professionals, and online dating sites as phatic toolkits designed to expand the reach of any single laborer. If contact can be conceptualized as "touching" or "touching together" (*fureai*, Nozawa

2015, 383–388), then we might think of phatic technologies like partner matching sites, or matchmakers' online databases, as cybernetic limbs that allow us fantastically expanded reach. The job of the matchmaker is, at its most basic, to introduce people. In the period immediately following WWII, matchmakers were typically volunteers who relied on personal networks to find the son or daughter of an acquaintance an appropriate spouse. The matchmaker's phatic labor would produce not only a durable relationship between husband and wife, but also between the matchmaking couple and the newlywed couple (Dore 1958, 168–169), and value would flow through this conduit as gifts to the matchmaker and obligations of material aid that either couple might render to the other in times of need. Now, value flows through the phatic conduits of matchmakers' labor and apps' structures as direct fees for services rendered, but the bond between the couple is also expected to be a conduit of value. Few people can ever really afford to live entirely alone, as celebrity matchmaker Yamada Yumiko points out in her blog and self-help books. Marriage, by virtue of expanding family connections and allowing for the birth of children, is a necessary kind of social insurance. She makes the connection between phatic labor as the producer of household labor (and value) with poignant clarity by, for example, creating a detailed checklist of all the social and material resources needed to live into old age single and cared for: savings or a pension sufficient to live on, health insurance, and adequate housing where one doesn't feel lonely (2009, 32).

Having now discussed the question of phatic labor more generally, we might ask what role gender plays in the organization of this work. Matchmakers perceive dramatic gender imbalances in communicative abilities and assumed communicative responsibilities. One reason for this is ideals of masculinity: whether he is shy or stoic (Alpert 2014), men are traditionally allowed to be *mukuchi*—literally, "without mouth." Silence has long been a valorized aspect of Japanese masculinity, although one that increasingly doesn't appeal to Japanese women. In describing the appeal of 1990s heartthrob Kimura Takuya, Fabienne Darling-Wolf notes that "Kimura's characters are the antithesis of the emotionless, distant, over-worked, unimaginative, sexist *salariman*—the dominant stereotype of late 20th century Japanese masculinity" (2003, 83). Kelsky (2001) and McLelland (2003) have argued that Japanese women's longing for both foreigners and gay men represents an important critique of Japanese masculinity: unlike Japanese men, Western men are characterized as chivalrous, egalitarian, and independent. Straight men are associated with abuse; gay men provide an imagined equality in relationships (McLelland 2003, 7). As an American woman studying in Japan, I remember clearly during one interview with a part-time matchmaker called Ozeki-sensei that, in a pause in our conversation, she expressed envy that as an American, I likely had experience dating wonderful Western men, who freely said "I love you." (Would, indeed, that my experiences had been so cinematic!)

If men are not talking, and not expressing their feelings, then phatic labor is effectively gendered: women are obliged to do it, and their fantasies, as described above, suggest that they resent it. During the course of my primary and continuing research on matchmaking, the uneven distribution of phatic labor has been a consistent theme. Between 2009–2011, the focus was on men as either too passive/herbivorous *or*, paradoxically, as too patriarchal. Regardless of the internal reasons for men's silence, both types of men would require their (female) partners to carry the conversation during introductions and dates. Attending Nakanishi Kiyomi-sensei's sessions during NNK meetings between 2015–2019 reveals that phatic problems linger, but are now discussed as technological ineptness along with conversational reticence. In the era of the smartphone, a perpetually open text chain with a loved one or a group of friends provides a venue for constant, routine, small acts of contact. In previous research, I have documented how matchmakers hold up the ability to effectively and proactively convey feelings verbally as essential to the project of matchmaking. Men's specific inability to do this has meant that men need to learn to communicate more like women, who are perceived as already being competently socialized and knowing how to make polite conversation (Alpert 2014, 204–205). In other words, men specifically need to become more effective phatic laborers, who are capable of sending daily texts, telling their partners how they feel about them, and otherwise keeping the conversation going. Just as Japanese women have turned to idealized images of foreign and gay men in order to critique their straight Japanese brethren for not doing their share of the housework, they also critique them for not doing their share of the conversational work of a relationship. Just as women must also learn to be assertive and declarative about their feelings, communicative coaching from matchmakers aims at equitably distributing conversational burdens by asking men to step up and contribute equally to the phatic labor that sustains relationships of all kinds.

In fact, matchmakers have developed a refined discourse about clients' phatic failures: it is, after all, their job. Online daters, however, report their own dissatisfactions. Writing a profile is a challenge, and interpreting one, an even greater challenge. But perhaps the greatest challenge of all is sending a message afterwards. Multiple interviewees described chains of interaction that look something like this, taken verbatim from a conversation my friend Ryan showed me on his phone and assured me was "*the* standard."

A: Hello

B: Hello

A: Thank you for matching with me. If it's good for you, please let's get to know each other.

B: Good evening, thank you to you too. Let's definitely get to know each other.

The conversation ends immediately after an exchange of ritual openings, greetings, and expressions of goodwill, all of which follow readily from each other, but do not then lead straightforwardly into a longer conversation. Having made all the required introductory talk, it's clearly someone's job to make the *second* move in order to continue the conversation, but no one seems to want to be responsible for it. Thus, two dating site users, having liked each others' profiles and greeted each other appropriately, simply let the conversation die. They then go on to match with someone else, and, often enough, conduct a nearly identical, equally unfruitful chat.

Ryan, a naturalized citizen of Japan who has almost exclusively dated in Japanese contexts, laid out the rules of messaging for me, according to his experiences with gay men on both dedicated gay apps and on Tinder. One Japanese-English term I've often heard for describing a good conversation is "catchball" (*kyatchi-bōru*)—basically, playing catch.[4] In a good conversation, like in a successful game of catch, one person throws the ball (an utterance), the other person catches it (listens), and then throws it back (formulates a reply)—and onward. Ryan noted that catchball-type, bouncing conversations often *fail* to happen because each person is trying to get the last word (or sticker, or emoji) in the conversation. They want their conversation partner to respond, but don't design their messages in a way that encourages the other person to respond in turn (for example, by answering one question and then asking the other person a new question). This puts the phatic burden of reaching out to continue the conversation onto the other person, who then has to decide whether or not to be vulnerable and put themselves out there in order to do so. Most times, the person on whom that burden falls chooses not to. In this instance, Ryan was excited about a prospective date because "he can send me a message without me having to do it for him. He can just send me a message because he wants to."

It's well worth noting that this problem of disclaiming one's own share of the conversational burden—this phatic skittishness—is not unique to Japan, nor is it a problem unique to men who date men. I've heard similar complaints from friends and research participants in English and Russian, in the United States and Kazakhstan, and from people of many genders and sexual orientations. In the matchmaking context, the professional consensus around phatic failures goes hand in hand with an analysis of gender in early twenty-first-century Japan. Conversations fail because

Japanese men don't know how to have them, because they are too shy or too manfully stoic to know how to contribute to a lively, shared conversation. By contrast, in online dating in Japan, my data contains some suggestions that men are too phatically *aggressive*, rather than inattentive or passive. In other words, men seem to have difficulty calibrating themselves phatically—targeting their contact carefully toward those who they are sincerely interested in, who are likely to be receptive to their communications, and communicating neither too much nor too little.[5] Zuckerman's concept of phatic violence reminds us that contact can be unwanted, harassing, distracting, and deleterious to the performance and well-being of those on the receiving end of it. I do not necessarily wish to impute nefarious motives to men who engage in what I am more mildly calling phatic aggression here. However, it is certainly true that this lack of calibration leads much contact from men within online dating spaces to have unpleasant effects on the women who receive unwanted attention.

In order to see how this works more specifically, let's look at an example from one of the first interviews that I conducted about online dating in 2018. Mika was a friend of a friend. She was in her twenties, and she had a boyfriend, but she nevertheless frequently browsed Tinder with her single friends as part of group conversations. Tinder's online dating mechanisms require both potential participants in a conversation to express interest in each other by "liking" each other's profiles before they "match" and are then able to send messages to each other within the app. Mika's firm belief was that men universally "liked" every profile displayed to them, so that *everyone* who returned the "like" would be available to them as a conversation partner. From there, they could pick and choose from a range of sure options, chatting only to women they were *really* interested in. She then demonstrated by swiping through profiles on Tinder while I watched. Every single profile that she "liked," time after time, came up as a match, without exception. She attributed this to men's flagrant abuse of the app, rather than assuming that no one could resist her profile.

I confess that men are somewhat underrepresented in my sample of interviewees, which is to say that only one of the three heterosexual men I interviewed told me that he did, indeed, "like" every profile in the way that Mika described. However, it certainly stands as proof that some men really do this. Moreover, the extent to which Tinder users worldwide engage in this sort of "like everyone" phatic splatter has been reflected in changes to the platform, which limit how many profiles a single user can "like" in a day—at least, for non-paying users (Crook 2015). In a qualitative analysis of sixty profiles from the konkatsu website Zexy Enmusubi, I found a bit of additional evidence of phatic splatter, suggesting that male users of this platform may also contact women fairly indiscriminately. A few women (four out of thirty) had various "disclaimers" on their profiles detailing types of men that they did *not* want to be contacted by: people too much older or younger, religiously observant people, people who live too far away, who don't post pictures of their faces, or who inflate their incomes to seem more attractive. No men's profiles, by contrast, had any such disclaimers. Men are thus apparently too quick to send messages to other users, and similar to the Tinder case, likely to send messages without really thinking about the other person, whether they really like them, or whether they might be suited to each other.

Communicating with new people is often awkward, in person or online—especially online. This is in part because these technologies are new, and disagreements about how to use them appropriately are widespread, a topic eloquently treated in Ilana Gershon's study of the role of new media in American breakups (2010). The significance of different communications may not lie so much in the words that former couples text or type to each other, but rather in how they switch between media, and which media are chosen for which kinds of communications (2020, 282). Breaking up with someone always hurts, but there's an extra layer to the pain when that breakup occurs via text message. What makes all of this especially poignant in Japan is that it occurs in the context of what seems like a society-wide phatic crisis. Nozawa (2015) characterizes phaticity in neoliberal Japan as an object of both fantasy and dread, using the local concept of *en* (connection, bond, karma). On the one hand, to be *mu-en*, without connections, can bring with it a joyous sense of release from social responsibility, along with the pleasure of no longer feeling like a burden to others (380–382). On the other hand, contemporary urban loneliness, and particularly, the neglect of the elderly, lead to a kind of phatic longing for any kind of contact at all, or the sense that one might mean something to another person by virtue of the simple fact of having been contacted. Here, Nozawa turns to the phrase *nanika no en*—"some kind of bond," or "fate"—to explain those glorious moments when one feels the pure joy of connection in unanticipated encounters. "Nanika no en" is at the root of "the fantasy of a pointy life," where one is not burdened by *tiresome* obligations, but *does* regularly feel rejuvenated, reinvigorated, reconnected by these dramatic points in life where "some kind of bond" brings a feeling of connection to someone, out of the blue (392–395).

FORMS OF CONTACT AND PHATIC TECHNIQUES

The point of all of this neoliberal phatic labor, from the perspective of the ordinary person commanded to engage in it, is to make first contact, create the foundation for lasting new connections, or perhaps, following

Nozawa, to uncover connections that seemed to just be there, waiting. For this purpose, both matchmakers and online daters have at their disposal a particular kind of phatic technology: the online profile. These profiles vary extensively. Matchmakers, regardless of which organizations they belong to, have a fairly fixed template for profiles. They are mostly text-based, with fields that contain all the information matchmakers argue are necessary for deciding basic compatibility with another person, or determining a potential mate's prospects in life. Naturally, they include information about the client: age, residence, hometown, height, weight, income (men only), level of educational attainment, and, in very broad terms, job (whether the person is self-employed, working in the private sector, in the public-sector, or in one of the professions). They also include information about the person's family, previous marriages (if any), children (if any), and finally, there is often a small blank space for a bit of personalization, labeled something like "self-promotion" (*jiko PR*) or "remarks" (*bikō*). There is also, of course, at least one picture of the client.

On dating sites, profiles vary more widely, in part because each site has its own architecture, its own gimmicks that distinguish it from other apps, and its own idea of what kind of people are (or should be) using the site to pursue what kinds of relationships. Tinder, for example, is relatively formless, with very few fields to fill in, and almost none of them mandatory except for name and age.[6] By contrast, konkatsu sites can be extremely detailed, including the kind of information that match-makers might focus on, but also perhaps expanding on that extensively, with any number of fields to fill in or boxes to tick to narrow down or specify very clearly what one might be looking for in a partner, along with space for some kind of self-introduction and—always—a profile photo. Rules about profile photos also vary substantially. Matchmakers, who exert much more control over their clients' profiles, will only upload reasonably high-quality pictures of their clients. In sharp but predictable contrast, on Tinder, a profile photo can literally be anything: a picture of a text quote, pets, landscapes, food, or seemingly random objects (all of which I have seen looking at Tinder profiles in Japan). And in yet another design, on Zexy Enmusubi, user-uploaded profile pictures must be approved by site staff before they can be displayed, and nearly every profile I have viewed has a clear picture of the user's face. Unlike matchmaking profiles, photos are not mandatory (but as discussed above, they are preferred). Zexy-Enmusubi also allows for uploading many pictures with prompts for different kinds of categories listed on top of grey, unfilled picture slots: a smile (*egao*), an upper-body shot (*jōhanshin*), a full-body shot (*zenshin*), a picture of the user engaged in a hobby (*shumi*), along with spaces for other potential kinds of pictures: landscapes, artistically-made lattes, basketballs, cats, bicycles, and plants.

Elsewhere (Alpert 2019), I have pondered the *conative* appeal of profile photos. The conative function of language is another of Jakobson's six functions, specifically, the function that focuses on the addressee of talk (1980). As an example, Jakobson gives the imperative mood—"call me!" We might also want to regard the vocative mood—"hey you!"—as another paradigmatic kind of conative language. A profile photo is not an utterance, or a text, but like conative language—like a command, a request, or a simple call out into the world—is designed around inciting a communicative response in the listener, in the same way as conative language. That desired response is very simple: "message me, pick me, want me, like me." This is also phatic, insofar as the command is to create a new connection, to respond to the profile in a way that enables users to begin to interact with each other.

The *language* of profiles is also phatic—notably more so in the purely online world, where users don't have access to matchmakers to give them advice or send along likely profiles. It is meant to introduce the user, tell the reader some basic things about them, and, classically, appeal to the reader in ways that, conatively and phatically, impel the viewer to make contact in some form or another, based on the affordances of particular interfaces. From my own extensive browsing, I remember that the English-language clichés of the late newspaper personals era in the United States were phrases like, "I enjoy candlelight dinners and walks along the beach." Such language, however trite in its image of romance, is nonetheless meant to give the reader a depiction of a possible—and hopefully desirable—future. While its tactics are completely different, the dry language of a Japanese matchmaking profile is also meant to allow the reader to picture what the future might be like with this person. Based on the displayed income, one might ask, "what kind of life could my partner and I live, with 10 million yen per year?" Based on information about family structure and residence, users might question whether they could live with a partner *and* their parents, too. Based on a description of someone's assets, like whether they already have a car or a house, apartment dwellers viewing that profile might wonder what it would be like to have homes of their own, and urbanites might ponder a move to the suburbs or the countryside with a car available. Motivated by desire for the futures they imagine, users reach out to others.[7]

As mentioned, within matchmaking systems, clients have to request an introduction from the other client, rather than simply liking them or messaging them, and starting a conversation from there. Online partner matching services and matchmaking in Japan both incorporate phatic systems that allow channels of communication to be established, with the difference being the presence or absence of human mediators. In the case of matchmaking, the initial contact between clients is mediated by their respective matchmakers. There is no direct conversation beforehand—rather, as soon as one client has accepted another's request to meet, the matchmakers arrange for a formal introduction (omiai) at everyone's earliest convenience so that their clients can have their first conversation in person. Direct communication between the clients begins at this introductory meeting. Matchmakers then check in with their clients afterward by asking them whether they'd like to see the other person again. If both consent, then each client receives other's contact information (phone number, email address), and from there, they are left more on their own to establish habits of communication, regular dates and texting, in order to determine whether they want to marry each other. However, the matchmakers are still there to give advice on communication (and anything else), and they can also step in to close the channel for breakups, just as they also opened it.

By contrast, those going it alone on the internet have no assistance from professionals, although the technological affordances of different applications may be more or less helpful in assisting users in some of the ways that a matchmaker might. All online partner matching technologies contain in-site or in-app methods of exchanging messages, so that two users can correspond and learn about each other before deciding to meet in person, or needing to exchange more personal contact information like phone numbers or social media profiles. Some systems are more limited than others. It may be that Tinder's most significant contribution to the world has been to introduce restrictions on messaging: two people can *only* message each other on Tinder if they indicate that they like each other (by "swiping right," using the app's famous gesture-based system of navigation). This has spread to some other platforms, like OKCupid, which introduced a similar system after Tinder rose to widespread popularity (Seppala 2017). A different app called Bumble, which has come up a few times in conversation with my interviewees, takes this even further, by barring male-identified users from messaging female-identified users first. That is, *first* both users must indicate interest in each other's profiles. After this, they can message each other, but in a heterosexual pairing, only the woman can start a conversation. Other online dating platforms may be unrestricted: anyone can send anyone else a message to express their interest.[8] Depending on the site, profile visibility settings may prevent the possibility of a match or a message. If a Tinder user changes their settings to only show other users within a 2-kilometer radius, for example, then even if someone with more expansive settings saw *their* profile, the first person will never see the profile of the person farther away, and thus, they will never match.

Additionally, some systems have multiple means of contact, with different levels of significance. For example, a number of sites have an option to send a user a "like": an indication of interest, a tentative check of communicative possibilities—something perhaps more delicate, or less frightening, than sending a message proper. Communication inherently makes us vulnerable to each other. Within sociolinguistics, some kinds of communication have been understood as entailing greater social and personal risks than others. Penelope Brown and Stephen Levinson (1987), in their classic work on politeness, call these *face-threatening acts*. A request, for example, exposes the vulnerabilities and needs of the person making it, who then risks "losing face," as it were. Likewise, the person who receives the request is also at risk of "losing face" by virtue of potentially having to turn the request down, and thereby seem ungenerous or uncaring. But these risks are not limited to requests alone. Ochs and Taylor (1995), in describing white American family dinnertime narratives, describe how, all too painfully, even the act of telling an ordinary story about one's day is embedded in gender orders and leaves the speaker's actions (particularly women's actions) open to "problematizing" and critique, particularly from husbands/fathers.

In order to mitigate the feeling of threat to self and other that face-threatening acts entail, speakers (of any and all languages) use a variety of politeness strategies to make the situation more "safe," by minimizing our requests, anticipating the denial of a request, or acknowledging the burden a request makes on its recipient (Brown and Levinson 1987, 61–71). "Liking" another user, then, is less threatening to both the sender and receiver. The receiver does not have to reply, since it is not a message per se. The sender has not imposed on the receiver, or exposed any deep feelings beyond mild interest. Some sites may even have a hierarchy of phatic options. The Japanese gay matching app *Nine Monsters*, for example, has a "like" option and a "message" option. Moreover, the app has a game component, featuring the titular nine monsters. Each user has a monster type assigned to them at the start. They can change their monster type and level up their profiles by "breeding" their monsters with other users'. In practice, according to Ryan, "breeding" is "a fancy like," whereas a "message shows much more interest/real effort." By choosing different phatic options, then, users can calibrate their attempts to open a communicative channel, by focusing either on minimizing risk through liking other users, or making a statement by sending a risky message—or perhaps waiting to send that message until after they receive a reciprocal like. On sites with restricted messaging options, the risk of sending a message is minimized by the structure of the app itself, since both users have already indicated their interest in each other.

Finally, another means of ensuring safety when making oneself vulnerable is the use of communicative strategies that reduce the sender's
uncertainty about the user they are sending a message to. In the case of
matchmaking, uncertainty reduction happens through the matchmaking system and the construction of the database. Clients can feel safe
meeting other clients because everyone in the database has been vetted
in person by a professional matchmaker. The phatic professionals have
already done the work of having initial conversations with their clients
to insure, for example, that they are seriously interested in marriage, or
that they seem like basically nice people that another matchmaker's client
could safely marry. The matchmakers that I've attempted to talk to about
online partner matching almost uniformly disapprove of the idea, given
that anyone can sign up and no one with a matchmaker's finely honed
intuition is checking who exactly these people are. Likewise, singles are
aware of the vulnerability inherent in potentially opening themselves up
to contact from strangers on the internet. A number of websites and apps
operating in Japan, aware of the need to reduce this feeling of vulnerability for their users, have built uncertainty reduction into the affordances
of their systems. So, for example, a number of online dating, koikatsu,
and konkatsu sites have embedded affordances for users to upload photographs of their personal identification, as well as giving their users the
option to search for *only* other users who have uploaded proof of identity.
(AirBNB, another service that exposes users to similar risks and vulnerabilities, also makes it possible to upload multiple forms of identification
along with other ways to verify users, for the exact same purposes.)

THE INTERSECTION OF POLITENESS,
GENDER, AND CONATIVE APPEAL

This chapter has attempted describe phatic language more generally,
and to show how phaticity is at the heart of both labor and technological
structures of online partner matching and neotraditional matchmaking in
Japan. In so doing, it has also looked at how language, phatic responsibility, and gendered ideas about both specific speech forms, and norms of
conversation, interact with each other. Along the way, I have forwarded
the notion that well-calibrated conversation in both matchmaking and
online datings favors an androgynization of conversational behavior,
with both men and women expected to clearly state their expectations
and desires while also empathizing with each other and working to keep
the conversation going.

In conclusion, I would like to return to this issue of androgyny, and
further explicate it, with reference to how gender intersects with norms

of politeness in Japanese, and strategies for managing conversational vulnerability. As previously mentioned, one of the major puzzles of my fieldwork was the near-complete absence of talk about gendered language, despite the fair mountain of literature on the subject of "Japanese Women's Language" and its well-established existence as a discrete and metapragmatically salient category of speech. My research on matchmaking and tour of online dating profiles has given me little to say about the use of specific grammatical forms that index dichotomous gender. Of course, we might be able to anticipate this result, since gendered forms have a more firm existence as ideological constructions rather than as real, locatable verbal styles in the speech of actual people. However, there is good reason to think that there is little formal gendered difference in the speech of male and female clients in matchmaking encounters, or on first dates. Some of this is due to the vulnerability of the encounter, the vulnerability of the whole endeavor of trying to find a partner, and the consequent attempt to try and reduce this vulnerability for all parties through the techniques of politeness. In Japanese, this means generally using addressee honorifics on verbs. It also means avoiding pronouns, or using relatively polite choices, when pronoun use is inevitable for clarity of writing or speech.

But politeness interacts with gender. Nakamura Momoko points out rather incisively that "Women's language is considered as a polite, soft, and feminine style of speaking, so female children are often told by their parents to speak more politely because they are women. Men's language is considered as a rough, direct, and masculine style, but no parents tell their sons to speak more roughly" (2014, 6). Polite language is gender-neutral, to some extent, or rather, when being polite, everyone speaks "women's language or standard Japanese." By contrast, "the use of men's language is restricted to a special situation in which a specific type of masculinity characterized by physicality, simplicity, violence, and aggressiveness . . . is emphasized" (2014, 7). While the Japanese *vox populi* characterizes women's language as uniquely gendered, and this gender distinction as a grand and unique Japanese tradition, Nakamura points out that most Japanese is spoken to a fairly "feminine" standard and, in fact, it is "men's language" that is the outlier.

And for good reason. Adhering to the rough, self-assertive stereotypes of "men's language" would be a poor move for a man meeting a prospective wife. Inasawa-sensei, a male matchmaker, emphasized to me the importance of showing *omoiyari*, which we might translate as "consideration," "sensitivity," "compassion," or "caring." Literally, the word means to give thought to something—to put oneself in another's position and imagine how they might feel, what they might want, and to act accordingly. Omoiyari can be demonstrated through (grammatically) polite speech and paying attention to one's interlocutor, imagining what she might want, or feel, or need, rather than taking a more "masculine" stance of aggression or assertiveness. Perhaps ironically, he told me that he learned this from his senior colleagues at work in a prior, more aggressive age of Japanese masculinity. They taught him that "women are always living in a dream," and that success with women was dependent on the ability to create a romantic dream for these women, or enter into one together.

As suggested by Brown and Levinson, politeness strategies are one of the ways that we extend this consideration to other people, reducing the perceived risks of certain kinds of interaction to both speakers and listeners. While I do not have data from actual conversations between matchmakers' clients, I do have data from looking at profiles on a number of different online platforms—and with very few exceptions, both men's and women's profiles adhere to a similar standard of politeness, with routine use of teineigo forms, but very little keigo. This is as true on more casual sites like Tinder as it is on gay men's hookup apps (Nine Monsters) and high-stakes konkatsu sites (Zexy Enmusubi, see also Alpert 2020). I would like to conclude by suggesting that there is a connection between empathy, androgyny, and phaticity in all partner matching endeavors. Politeness, rather than highly gendered language, is part of the phatic design of these processes, and is part of what smoothes the way to opening new connections through profiles, likes, messages, and meetings. Phaticity depends on being able to imagine the other person's subject position—to transmit, as it were, on a shared wavelength—in anticipation of others' vulnerabilities and desires.

NOTES

1. A practice still maintained by OKCupid, which remains a popular website in the US.

2. There is some regional variation to take into account here; what is "soft" in Tokyo is often appropriate for men in the west of Japan. SturtzSreetharan 2006a and 2006b provide more linguistic detail.

3. "The Problem of Meaning in Primitive Language" is the title of Malinowski's 1923 piece where he develops the concept of "phatic communion." See Malinowski 1946.

4. See also Alpert 2014 for a discussion of "catchball" in heterosexual marriage bureau advising.

5. I am grateful to the anonymous reviewer of this manuscript who suggested this interpretation.

6. Paying for the privilege can allow some Tinder users to hide even their age, and of course, there are no Facebook-style requirements that the name be anything, especially honest or revealing.

7. Here, I owe a significant theoretical debt to Daniel Miller's *A Theory of Shopping* (1998), which analyzes consumption behavior in relation to consumers' imagined futures—for example, purchasing new furniture in the hope of having guests over more, or buying groceries while thinking about the health and happiness of family members.

8. Depending on the site and the niche it occupies in the online partner matching landscape, "anyone" may be—and often is—limited by gender. Konkatsu sites in Japan operate under a strict presumption of heterosexuality, which makes sense, given that Japanese law at present only allows heterosexual marriages. On Zexy Enmusubi, for example, it's impossible for users who indicate that they are men to search or view other men's profiles, let alone send them messages.

3

✛

Inventing and Reinventing Matchmaking as Phatic Entrepreneurship

Very little has been written about matchmaking or brokered marriage in Japan in the scholarly literature, neither in Japanese nor in English. Perhaps this is because, for a time, arranged marriages, assisted by go-betweens called nakōdo (仲人, literally, "relationship people"), were tremendously ordinary things. Then, rather swiftly after the end of the Second World War, they became increasingly unusual. However, both the obvious and the unusual hold tremendous promise for ethnographers. The unusual can help us draw out and test the boundaries of human possibility. It can show us what can form the basis of a functional and content existence, for individuals and societies, even if what we find might seem surprising. Moreover, it holds up a mirror to the obvious, showing us that what seems natural in any given society has always been constructed, and, therefore, could have been constructed another way, or could *still be* reconstructed. By contrast, investigating the obvious in detail shows us how it is that we go about actually constructing obviousness, making "human nature" out of social convention. But the obvious rarely turns out to actually be as obvious as it seems, and the world of the "natural," "normal," and "obvious" exists more in the subjunctive than the indicative mood. We look at the "obvious" to find ideals, and the "unusual" to see how those ideals are negotiated in practice.

So, it is with marriage and matchmaking in Japan, its recent history, and its contemporary permutations. In the mid-twentieth century, approximately half of all Tokyo marriages could be characterized as "arranged" in some way (Blood 1967). But the past has become a foreign country, and consequently, an arranged marriage often sounds about as exotic to today's Japanese adults in their twenties and thirties as it does to many outside Japan. Most people that I've casually talked with about my research over the years will say that arranged marriages used to be "the Japanese way" of doing things, for some period of time, in some not clearly specified past. Some, like my good friend Marie, may even have parents whose marriage was arranged, and thus may have more personal experience with the topic. In fact, Marie's current partner, who is foreign and actually terribly embarrassed about having met her through Tinder, credits Marie's total comfort with meeting people online to her own parents' arranged marriage. Even then, unless they have personal connections of some kind to the marriage industry, few are aware of the extent to which matchmaking has transformed, become a service industry, and as such, continues into the present day—even though the share of marriage it occupies has more or less steadily decreased.

The transformations in the commonality of arranged marriages and actual practices of singles, families, and matchmakers, lead us to several questions. First of all, how did matchmaking become "normal," and then, what changed? How did matchmaking become outdated? Given that it is now so outdated and unusual, why would someone still participate in it today? Finally, what is the actual job of a matchmaker in the twenty-first century, and how has it transformed along with attitudes toward matchmaking? While I provide a brief historical overview of the practice of arranged or brokered marriage, this chapter focuses primarily on that last question. Here we will look at the practicalities of matchmaking as a job, the way matchmakers receive formal and informal job training, and the collective conventional wisdom that they develop, pass on to new matchmakers, and also teach their clients about how to find a marriage partner. We can conceptualize matchmakers' work generally as a type of phatic labor. This labor produces a number of concrete results, including income for matchmakers, reputational proof of their effectiveness—which also serves as a form of advertising—and emotional satisfaction for themselves and hopefully their clients. All of this is, of course, in addition to the obvious new phatic connections being forged between clients who may become husbands and wives.

INVENTING AND REINVENTING MATCHMAKING

Historians have located the rise of many "Japanese traditions" in the late nineteenth and early twentieth centuries. As products of modernity, rather than antiquity, they have often characterized them as "invented traditions," (Hobsbawm and Ranger 1983, cited in Vlastos 1998). The practices that historians call "invented traditions" were in no way wholly new at the time they were canonized as "traditional." Rather, while they existed, they did not exist in the same way, were not practiced in the same way, were not distributed through society in the same way. They may have been practices restricted to a particular region, group, or time period, but once they were codified as "tradition," they became regarded as the property and duty of the whole modern Japanese nation. Vlastos gives the Japanese "spirit of peace and harmony" (6) and the sport of sumo (7), as examples of "invented traditions," among others.

Before the nineteenth century, some marriages in Japan were certainly arranged. Hendry (2017, 107–108) notes that while "the common people" usually married according to free choice, samurai families making strategic alliances might need to employ the services of a go-between. But, as a society-wide practice, matchmaking seems to be another kind of "invented tradition," largely established during the Meiji period (1868–1912), when the emperor was restored to political power; Japan had only recently been forced to initiate trade with the United States and Europe, and the country was embarking on a campaign of rapid modernization and Westernization. The new Meiji government, determined to abolish feudal ways, did away with the official, rigid class system of warriors, farmers, artisans, and merchants that characterized the preceding Tokugawa period (1603–1868). As a result, one feature of this period of rapid social change is that class-specific, aristocratic practices often became simply "Japanese" (Sakai 2009). Even then, they took some time to filter through the populace at large, and truly became generalized. Smith and Wiswell (1982), in their account of the lives of village women in Japan prior to WWII, tell us that in early modern Japan, outside of the samurai class, most young Japanese people had substantial freedom to experiment sexually and choose their own partners. This freedom persisted in rural Japan for decades after official ideologies began to promote family authority, virginity before marriage, and monogamy afterwards; Wiswell collected her data in the 1930s.

The invented tradition of brokered marriage was, for a time, extremely successful and indeed, extremely widespread. Arranging marriages with the help of nakōdo was the dominant marriage practice in Japan from the late nineteenth century until sometime after the Second World War. In his mid-twentieth-century ethnography of urban Tokyo (1958), Ronald Dore was able to articulate some of these norms around marriage and matchmaking, which at the time was still widespread. For the majority of couples in his study, go-betweens were involved in arranging a marriage, whether they introduced the couple in the first place, or came in later to negotiate the economic aspects of what began as a love match. In most cases, partners knew very little about the other beforehand, although at the time of Dore's study, they might be encouraged to get to know each other after a formal first meeting, the omiai. In the case of wholly arranged marriages, refusing one's chosen partner after the omiai was possible, but incredibly awkward and socially difficult. The nakōdo of this period were not paid *per se*, but they did receive extensive and expensive gifts for their services. Nakōdo were also incorporated ritually into the wedding ceremony, and typically kept in touch with couples long after their marriage. Dore also noted that couples and go-betweens would often help each other out economically in difficult times (1958, 165–169): the bond between nakōdo and newly married couple was meaningful and durable. We can also see this in one of Nana Okura Gagné's life histories of a salaryman working for the same company both before and after the economic reforms of the 1990s and 2000s. Gagné tells us that her interviewee, Takagi-san, eventually married via omiai in 1978. However, he had outright refused an offer of matchmaking assistance some years earlier from his particularly passionate and strict boss, who viewed being a matchmaker for someone as becoming functionally another parent to that person, capable of exercising additional authority over them. Takagi-san, who was already overwhelmed by his boss, was wary of inviting the man any further into his life (2020, 194–200).

If matchmaking was such a successful invention, one might very reasonably ask, why did matchmaking subsequently become *unpopular*? To some extent, at least, we can point to Western, specifically American, influence and intervention in Japanese law and social structure. The post-war Japanese constitution, written by American Occupation forces, mandated that marriage take place only between two mutually consenting parties; previously, the head of household had also been required to give his consent to a marriage (Steiner 1950). This legal change gave Japanese young people, especially young women, a kind of personal freedom unheard of under earlier Japanese law. These legal changes were accompanied by cultural changes around courtship and sex, again under American sway. The erotic influence of the occupying forces made practices such as public kissing, casual sex, and Western-style dating seem fun, new, and democratic (McLelland 2010). As described by Mark McLelland, this influence was exerted visually, as American couples held hands in the streets and romantic American movies entered Japanese popular culture. However, it was also experienced viscerally, as many Japanese women entered into erotic and marital relationships with American soldiers.

As the second half of the twentieth century progressed, love matches became *de rigeur*. Relationship styles and modes of expressing intimacy and affection that were liberatory seventy years ago have now become normal and expected. National survey figures from the Japanese National Institution of Population and Social Security Research (NIPSSR) show clearly that the percentage of "love matches" versus "arranged marriages" has steadily declined since the end of the war, and the percentage of arranged marriages currently seems to be holding steady at around 5.3 percent of the total (2016, 12).[1] Sociologist Anthony Giddens, in describing the history of romantic love in the West, characterized the most recent forms of intimacy in late capitalist societies as a move from relationships based on romance, and toward what he called "pure" relationships, motivated solely by a desire to be with one's partner, absent economic or household considerations (1992, 58). In Japan, too, there seems to be an increasing desire for this kind of "pure relationship." One woman that I interviewed, in her mid-forties, was in the middle of looking for a partner herself, while simultaneously training to become a matchmaker. She commented to me that:

> Having an omiai, meeting who your parents told you to, getting married, having children, that was happiness for women, but now, that, umm, in an age where we self-actualize so much, umm, uh just having children, the thinking is, that isn't a life, that thinking has really spread, hasn't it?

Higashi-san's words indicate that self-actualization is now more important than simply fulfilling a set life course, and that marriage is something to be considered in terms of whether and how it serves individuals. At the same time, there seems to be a certain amount of reflection within Japanese popular and academic culture on whether postponing marriage and childbearing, emphasizing career, single life, and self-actualization, have actually served young Japanese men and women well. One consequence is that the invented tradition of brokered marriage has undergone a process of reinvention in order to seem relevant to a society that now embraces—however awkwardly—the idea that marriage is ultimately a free association between individuals. It has done this in part by linking itself to the neoliberal discourse of konkatsu: the phatic labor of seeking to forge new connections leading to marriage.

The contemporary, neoliberal instantiation of matchmaking emphasizes the importance of marriage, but within a framework of individual responsibility and choice. Today's matchmakers do not choose partners for their clients, although they may suggest people to meet, or profiles to look at. It might be better to say that matchmakers serve as a *medium*, in multiple senses, for meeting new people. To some extent, as phatic professionals, matchmakers form part of the communicative channel connecting new clients with each other in interaction and prospective relationship. The matchmaker is there to help clients meet new people and, in subsequent steps, to help the client actively steer a budding relationship toward success (which is defined as engagement and marriage). Generally speaking, the matchmakers I worked with believe that anyone can get married, just as they did in the past, if only they are willing to follow their matchmaker's advice about self-presentation, communication, and the best ways to cultivate mutual feeling and express emotions.

I use the word "feeling" instead of "love" for several reasons. One of those is simply that *kimochi*, usually translated "feeling," was the most common word used by matchmakers to describe what couples should aim to develop as they date and decide whether to marry. It can embrace emotions as deep as love, but need not denote more than sufficient affection to marry—however much or little that may be. This brings me to the second reason, which is that matchmakers disagree about whether love and marriage have anything to do with each other at all. A certain degree of mutual feeling is indispensable, and must be cultivated. Love (*ren'ai, aijō*), however, is not. Thus, in addition to teaching their clients about *how* to catch a spouse, they are also trying to lower clients' expectations about what marriage requires of people, and thus, lower their resistance to an institution that seems to require unbearable sacrifice with an impossible-to-find sort of partner.

One intriguing thing about the matchmakers' discourse is that within it, feelings become deliberate practices instead of internal experiences or static mental states—again, this makes them accessible and possible for everyone. Despite matchmakers' ambivalence about love, they also frequently claim that couples who marry through omiai seem as in love with each other as any other couple at their weddings. According to the decidedly unromantic Nakao-sensei,

> Clients often ask, "Teacher, um, how do you decide on marriage?" They say that, right? "You know," I say. "It's OK if it's not awful when you're together." I tell them, "It's OK if you don't fall in love. Once you're married? You know? After all just being together brings forth bonds, feeling. So that, you know? There's no place for anything like love in marriage."

And yet, when it comes down to it:

> As they turn towards marriage and start different kinds of preparation, of course they grow close, and of course they're going to become at the wedding like, the kind of couple that makes you think "They really fell in love, didn't they?"

The practice of being a couple, for Nakao-sensei, is what creates the emotional content necessary for marriage, rather than the other way around. Similarly, Miyamoto-sensei commented that "love is in the process" of getting married, rather than being the starting point for a marriage. Over the last twenty years, one strand of research on language, gender, and sexuality has focused on the instantiation of "desire" or "love" through language use (Kulick 2000; Cameron and Kulick 2003). In these accounts, desire is not something that simply happens, but rather something that is created performatively, citationally, through the use of familiar romantic tropes in language. Laura Ahearn (2002) describes the introduction of literacy in rural Nepal as one such circumstance. Discourses of development in Nepal created further discourses of the need to self-actualize, in part through the independent choice of a romantic partner, as opposed to an arranged marriage. At the same time, the introduction of literacy as a technology also enabled young lovers to communicate away from the surveillance of friends and family, thus using linguistic means to accomplish this self-actualization. Desire was fueled through words, often taking the form of stereotyped declarations of love and passion that followed the advice of guidebooks produced precisely for these young letter writers. A letter was recognizable as a love letter precisely because it followed the newly established form of one.

There are a number of parallels to be made here with the work of contemporary Japanese matchmakers. Matchmakers' main job is to give their clients advice, not just on how to select a partner, but on how to communicate with that partner, during omiai and while dating, in order to create the desire to see each other again, spend more time together, get to know each other, and ultimately, get married. Matchmakers do not try to help their clients find love, but to help them create it. Desire is not only created interactionally, but it is also sustained interactionally. Similarly, modern kinship studies tend to focus on how kin relationships are created and sustained through shared experiences, rather than taking for granted the existence of predetermined familial relationships. Janet Carsten's key work (1995) describes the creation of kin relationships in Langkawi, Malaysia, through food, which becomes blood, and thus bodily substance. As a result, people who live in a house and share routine meals become functionally, *biologically*, "the same," which is to say, they become kin. Krista van Vleet's account of kinship in the Andes (2008) demonstrates that what kin share need not be physical, like food or blood, but can instead be shared narratives that display and construct relationships. Laura Miller (1997) suggests that the proliferation of personality typing exercises and divination schemata in women's magazines helped women to cope with the "anxiety" caused by a proliferation of life course choices that departed from the earlier expectation of being introduced to a spouse at an appropriate age and beginning domestic life. Instead, they could understand themselves as a particular kind of "type" with particular needs and desires and compatibilities and foibles. This helped them to create their own romantic narratives, and perhaps also, to explain why they might deviate from older norms of being a good bride (*o-yome-san*). The o-yome-san is supposed to assimilate to her new family's ways, and then independently manage her sphere of the corporate "household" (*ie*), long seen as the defining structure of Japanese kinship (Kitaoji 1971, Faier 2009).[2] For matchmakers, what clients need in order to build marriage bonds is time and talk, repeated meetings and solicitations wherein they get to know each other, discuss their expectations for a future, married life, and build up a relationship in the process—in other words, create a narrative for their life together, much as Miller theorized for magazine readers.

In so doing, successful clients are not only instantiating romantic desires and feelings in their partners, but also acting on and realizing their own desires for the kind of lifestyle that they believe marriage has to offer them. According to the NIPSSR, 35.8 percent of single Japanese men and 49.8 percent of women want to get married in order "to have their own children and family," while 31.1 percent and 28.1 percent of men and women respectively anticipate that it will bring them "psychological relief." Women, in particular, also seek marriage for "financial stability" (2016, 2). Enacting romantic desire therefore becomes inextricably bound up in the simultaneous construction of the self and the other as desirable partners and people, and as the keys to a desirable life—the father or mother of longed-for children, the partner who eases one's burdens. This is carried out through the multiparty interaction of clients and their matchmakers, and through the different scenes of omiai, dating, and counseling between matchmakers and clients.

THE MARRIAGE INDUSTRY

It is somewhat difficult to discern just how many people are actually participating in konkatsu of some kind. This is especially true given that, consonant with the neoliberal imagination of the self as a set of sellable skills (Urciuoli 2008), many forms of self-improvement have been characterized as "konkatsu" insofar as they might raise one's potential value on the marriage market. Psychologist Shibuya Shozo, in his guide to konkatsu etiquette, uses survey data from Match.com to discuss men's and women's different konkatsu strategies. Signing up with marriage introduction offices (*kekkon shōkai-jo*) was a top strategy for both women and men, along with "dating," "omiai," and "asking for introductions from friends." Although women were more likely to prefer more formal strategies (like using marriage introduction services or omiai), Shozo argues that men largely try to informally increase their contact and communication with women. Additionally, women often try to improve their domestic skills, take more care with their fashion, read books to "polish their inner beauty" and both men and women expressed concern with "increasing their economic power," in terms of both saving money and increasing income (2009, 40–41). Perhaps the most dramatic example of the vagaries of what qualifies as konkatsu would be my friend Yuri, who once told me she was doing "mental" (*nōnai*) konkatsu.[3] The implication is that getting married requires active effort in terms of meeting eligible partners, whether through formal or informal channels—but being the kind of person who possesses the skills and assets necessary for a comfortable married life *also* requires active effort. It's not enough to find a partner, but to be prepared, mentally, financially, domestically, and intellectually for marriage.

Of all of the people who have engaged in some kind of konkatsu since the word was coined in 2008, the number engaged specifically in *matchmaking* is decidedly small. Nakanishi Keiji estimated at an Osaka NNK member's meeting in November 2010 that only about 3 percent of single Japanese men and women make use of marriage bureaus, matchmakers, or similar neotraditional partner matching services. Given the statistics on the popularity of arranged marriages, the number has probably not substantially increased over the last ten years, although matchmakers have certainly been advertising heavily. At the same time, Japan is not a small country. While 3 percent is a tiny fraction of the population, there are still literally thousands of marriage services, small and large, all across Japan. Not all of them are willing to disclose their numbers. However, O-net, a nationwide partner matching service, claimed to have 27,534 male and 20,473 female clients as of January 1, 2021, while noting that this number also includes 12,868 people who had temporarily suspended their memberships for reasons of pursuing relationships or other personal circumstances.[4] IBJ, a Japanese national federation of individual matchmakers, claimed around 70,295 clients as of April 2021, with 2,767 individual marriage bureaus in its network.[5] The NNK is somewhat smaller in scope than IBJ, with more small-scale, part-time matchmakers in its ranks—1,800—and only around ten thousand clients as of July 2018,[6] although it is increasingly professionalizing and expanding. Omiai may have declined substantially over the course of the twentieth and twenty-first centuries, but in a country as populous as Japan, the raw numbers of people using various matchmaking services are still substantial.

As mentioned previously, the word "omiai" itself is an honorific noun that literally means "seeing together" or "see and meet." There is a tremendous amount of cultural significance and weight attached to this word, given that the Japanese term for *arranged* marriage is actually *omiai* marriage (*omiai kekkon*). A century ago, once a couple was introduced at an omiai, the match was more or less made. Ethnographic reports also tell us that in times past (the increasingly distant early to mid twentieth century), parents were much more involved in the omiai process (Vogel 1961;

Blood 1967; Hendry 1981). Even today, parents may still arrange omiai privately. I have been frequently asked whether anything like omiai exists in the United States; my usual response has been that although there are few true matchmakers, parental meddling is universal. Sayo, a friend of a friend, sat down with me one day to talk about her own experience with her parents insisting on an omiai. A son of a friend of a friend of her father's wanted to meet any of his daughters, and ultimately, Sayo was the one who couldn't get out of the obligation, even though she had a boyfriend at the time. She protested that it would be rude for her to go if her partner was taking it seriously, but she was already certain she would refuse him. However, her mother insisted she do it anyway, "for the experience." During the actual omiai, Sayo said that she was nervous, but about disappointing her mother, not about impressing the man she was meeting.

Although this particular omiai was never going to be a success because of circumstances entirely external to it, Sayo's case demonstrates that the association of omiai with parental authority and Japanese traditions remains strong. However, in actual practice, any number of mediating individuals or even corporations may stand in the role of "matchmaker," and the process of arranging and conducting an omiai may involve a variety of different practices. As currently practiced, "seeing together" is all the contemporary omiai really aims to do. Most contemporary omiai are relatively casual meetings arranged for the purpose of introducing a single man and a single woman to see how they get on. They are something like a screen test—an opportunity to see if some kind of phatic connection can be forged, or again in theatrical terms, to see if there is any "chemistry." This brings us back to one of the goals of this chapter, which is simply to describe what matchmaking is like as a job, and where matchmakers fit in the larger sphere of Japan's marriage industry, many sectors of which use both the "traditional" language of omiai and nakōdo, and the modern language of konkatsu. The goal here is not to delineate who are the *real* nakōdo, although the matchmakers I worked with certainly have strong opinions on the subject. The matchmaker's anachronistic job title and self-styling is meant to signal a different and more personal business model than many of the larger businesses on the scene, which are also building on imagined Japanese marriage traditions. Using terms like nakōdo is a recursive differentiating technique, where, according to Irvine and Gal (2000), differences in one domain are meant to index differences in another domain. Here, older language is meant to point to an older style of partner matching, by virtue of their shared old-fashioned resonance.

This is not to suggest that there are not genuine differences between matchmakers and other areas of the marriage business. This is true even though online portals for signing up and searching for partners are nearly ubiquitous in the marriage industry; email, text, and LINE messages dominate communication in every domain; and terminology supposedly belonging to the most conservative branches of the marriage industry has spread to everywhere else. Regardless of whether or not the matchmakers I worked with would consider all meetings arranged through these various services to be proper "omiai," using the term evokes the safety and legitimacy of tradition, while the web portals for all of these services, covered with romantic Western-style bridal imagery, promise clients the convenience of the new and the romance of *romance*. So what, then, differentiates the matchmakers that I worked with as a legitimately separate sphere of the broader partner matching and marriage industry? As one example, nearly every self-described nakōdo that I interviewed was self-employed as such, although they typically join matchmaker associations like the aforementioned IBJ or NNK in order to have access to a shared client database. Some may also work in teams with other matchmakers, learning from the senior matchmakers and helping to handle client overflow. For example, I first met Sugawara-sensei as a member of Yasuda-sensei's team. She later struck out on her own but, when I last encountered her during fieldwork in the summer of 2019, she had returned to work in a larger marriage-bureau environment. Married couples or family members might also work together, sharing clients, introduction, and advising duties. In all cases, businesses remain small.

Another meaningful difference can be found in their pricing schemes. Larger organizations tend to charge large, comprehensive fees at signup, but O-net's website, for example, proudly advertises the fact that they don't charge a *seikonryō*, or "successful marriage fee." By comparison, the NNK bylaws limit the amounts that member matchmakers are allowed to charge for introductory fees to ¥30,000.[7] These introductory fees are used largely to maintain the clients' records with the matchmaker associations. They support the technological infrastructure of the association's database, and the association staff who maintain it. In other words, matchmakers earn little to no money when they sign up clients. According to Nakanishi Keiji, their main income—in theory—comes precisely from the seikonryō, which they receive from clients when they get engaged. Based on matchmaking contracts that I have seen, this fee is usually around ¥100,000–¥300,000. A matchmaker *can* be as expensive as a large marriage information service, but *only* for those clients who succeed and get married, and never up front. As a result of this difference in pricing, as well as differences in business organization, matchmakers are theoretically more motivated to be active on their clients' behalf, preparing them to meet new people, and pushing them forward toward marriage. The logic is not unlike that of jobs in high-stakes sales—real estate, for example—that pay entirely or primarily by commission.

Large businesses generally leave "omiai" entirely up to the clients themselves (which might lead one to ask how an omiai is different to a date, or what the difference is between online konkatsu and online dating). Matchmakers, however, work in public, and their omiai are visible to anyone who knows where to go and what to look for. I am not certain how staff at larger marriage businesses learn how to do their jobs, but they have the employment infrastructure of a sizable company looking after them, and training them to meet certain goals. However, these goals may serve the businesses more than the clients. At the Osaka NNK members' meeting in June 2019, one matchmaker addressed the group about her substantial career in the marriage industry, which included stints as an event organizer, a counselor at one of the large matching services, and eventually, an independent matchmaker who joined the NNK. In her speech, she harshly criticized the training and incentives provided to employees at these organizations: no clients were turned away, regardless of their chances at finding someone, and awards for best employees were largely based on the number of contracts they convinced clients to renew, that is, the amount of money they brought in. As a result, she became profoundly disillusioned with an industry that made it seem like marriage was actually a bit beside the point.

By contrast, the individual matchmaker has no such infrastructure, and this is another difference between the nakōdo I primarily worked with, and other marriage industry players. When an individual nakōdo has questions about the job, they have to be answered experientially, or through collaboration with and advice from other matchmakers. As a result, what matchmakers have to say comes out of a mix of idiosyncratic opinion and amorphous collective wisdom that answers questions such as, How should matchmakers network professionally? How should they communicate with each other and collectively provide a professional assessment of the state of marriage and non-marriage in Japan today? How do they understand the reasons that clients don't, can't, or won't get married? How do they come to an understanding of what Japanese men and women expect from each other in marriage? Largely, they teach each other the basics of the profession: how to counsel clients, how to help write and evaluate profiles, and how to serve as communicative intermediaries—phatic laborers and phatic conduits—whose job it is to transmit clients' desires to each other, and to facilitate both introductions and breakups. They do this through a mix of formal and informal structures: matchmaker associations, professional observation and partnership, and friendship.

EDUCATING BOTH MATCHMAKERS
AND CLIENTS IN THE MATCHING ARTS

In this section, I discuss the basic content that matchmakers need to learn to do their jobs, as well as how they learn it. The most basic task of the matchmaker is to "keep" (*azukaru*) clients, and to introduce them to likely candidates for marriage. "Introduction" has both the sense of helping clients find someone appropriate, by perhaps sending along the profiles of likely partners, as well as actually conducting the omiai where the two prospective marriage candidates meet. As both Yasuda-sensei and Inasawa-sensei explained to me in my first interviews with them in 2009 and 2010, they see themselves as operating in an unbroken line with the community elders—the bosses at work and the neighborhood grand-mothers of Dore's ethnography—who would be asked to arrange marriages for young people because of their authority in the community.[8] In this unspecified past, matchmakers would be able to pair couples up on their own, in part because the populations they were dealing with were considerably smaller, and in part because, having asked a matchmaker for assistance, it might have been too rude to refuse whatever partner the matchmaker suggested.

Things are very different now, and one of the first things that match-makers learn about is the flow of the modern omiai system. While matchmakers' central responsibility is conducting introductions, this may actually be the least time-consuming of their professional activities. And if, in the past, marriage was mostly a foregone conclusion after the omiai, in the current professional system the omiai is but one step in a longer process. This basic process was described to me during my preliminary fieldwork by Miyamoto-sensei and Kawakami-sensei, and I have since seen it laid out on a variety of different websites and elaborated in NNK training seminars in more or less the same form. The process begins when the client and matchmaker meet, discuss the process and the paperwork, and the matchmaker evaluates the client. This evaluation consists of two parts. The first is whether the client is sincere in their desire to get mar-ried, and generally, the kind of person a matchmaker might want to intro-duce to other clients. Webb Keane describes sincerity as "not just a matter of imputed alignment between expression and interior state but also a product of one's desire to make one's expressions aligned in this way." But, in addition to this, in order to convey this alignment between exter-nal words and internal thoughts, a person who wishes to seem sincere has to demonstrate it socially in some way: "sincerity is a kind of public accountability to others for one's words, with reference to oneself" (2007, 211). It is not entirely clear how matchmakers determine this sincerity in their initial encounters with potential clients—it is a task left up to the matchmaker's instincts.

However, more broadly, matchmakers tend to regard conversational style and conversational ability as indices of a persons's inner self. For example, a handout from the NNK, "*Omiai no Kokoro-e*" ("Omiai Knowledge"), states in its section on "Conversation and Attitude" (*kaiwa to taido*):

> From beginning to end, let's be bright and clear and smiling. Let's emphasize the inner self as much as outward appearances, and try to find a good side to things. Just answering questions, falling silent, sitting with bad posture and constantly looking at others, things like that are ridiculous. Even if your partner isn't someone you like, please don't do anything rude that shows in your attitude. Let's always keep enjoyable topics in mind.

Here, paralinguistic information (facial expression) and conversational style (attentive, pleasant) "emphasizes the inner self," which ought to be positive, considerate of others' feelings, and cooperative in the mutual endeavor of conversation.

If both matchmaker and client are satisfied with each other, then the client might sign all the paperwork and pay the introductory fees at their initial meeting, or at a subsequent meeting, after having time to think. The next step is creating a profile. These usually follow a standard template for each association's database, and each association's database is a little bit different, but profiles typically feature similar factual information about clients. Unlike online dating profiles, there is very little in the way of free text fields. NNK profiles have one free text field, labeled "remarks" (*bikō*), which is to be filled in sparingly, but artfully. The client supplies the information, and the matchmaker helps the client massage the information into the most flattering shape the form allows, which the matchmaker ultimately enters into an online database owned by the matchmaker association that they belong to on the client's behalf.[9] In some cases, where matchmakers belong to multiple organizations, the profile may be entered into multiple databases. This was what happened when Kawakami-sensei took me on as an informal client. After filling out a paper form with all the information needed for the profile, she and her partner entered it in, and then she sent me two sites to log into, with two sets of login information, and two databases to search. I confess that I was extremely confused about this for a long time. It hadn't occurred to me that matchmakers might belong to multiple organizations until the subject came up at an NNK meeting. It makes sense, however, that some individual matchmakers might try to extend their reach as far as possible by connecting themselves to multiple infrastructures.

Once clients have access to the database(s), then, with their matchmakers' guidance, they can browse and search people of the opposite sex that they might wish to meet, and can also apply online to meet them. Clients are also able to receive requests from other clients in the database. Most neotraditional matchmaking is strictly heterosexual, and it is only upon engagement that matchmakers receive their biggest payout, the "successful marriage fee." The databases are constructed so that male clients can only search for female clients, and vice-versa. There are a few exceptions.[10] Some konkatsu agencies aimed at the LGBTQ+ community now exist. These are doubtless responses to the growing recognition of same-sex marriage by local governments beginning with Shibuya and Setagaya Wards in Tokyo in 2015 (Ito and Lim 2015), even prior to March 2021's ruling by the Sapporo district court (Kobayashi and Hollingsworth 2021). But at the time that I conducted the majority of my research, none of this was on the horizon, and it is still true today that most konkatsu services and sites retain the rigidly heteronormative approach that I encountered during my fieldwork.

When a client sends a request to meet, the receiving party must either accept or refuse it within a delimited time span (for the NNK, this is about two weeks). If the request is accepted, then the omiai must be arranged, with matchmakers mediating the discussion on behalf of their clients to arrange a suitable date, time, and location for all four parties (the man, the woman, and both their matchmakers). Omiai are typically conducted in public spaces like hotel lobbies. So far as I can discern—because no one has ever told me outright—the rationale for the hotel lobby seems to be that hotels are public and safe, and moreover, somewhat formal locations, with nice (and often expensive) cafés and restaurants, and impressive marble decor. Moreover, many major hotels are located near major train junctures, such as Kyoto Station in Kyoto, or Umeda or Nanba in Osaka, so it's usually easy for everyone to find their way to the appointed meeting place. Once everyone has gathered (the two clients, and ideally, both of their matchmakers), the matchmakers conduct formal introductions and, depending on their schedules and their attitudes to omiai, the matchmakers may either send the couple off on their own for coffee, or sit down with them for a bit to get the conversation started. The restaurants and cafés provide a built-in, quiet place to which the couple can retire immediately following their introduction—or if those spaces are occupied, the busy surrounding area will offer many choices for casual tea and cake.

Following the omiai, each client reports back to their matchmaker after a day or two to discuss how things went, and whether they would be interested in seeing the other person again. If either of the two clients says "no," then nothing else happens. No relationship can follow; the connection is severed. Each client starts the process over again, having ruled each other out. However, if *both* say they want to see each other again, then they move from the omiai phase to the *kōsai* (dating) phase of the matchmaking process. The matchmakers exchange their clients' contact information, and pass them on to the clients so they can communicate with each other directly. During kōsai, clients are supposed to see each other at least once per week, if not more frequently, and maintain a regular correspondence over email, phone, and text as well. While matchmaker mediation is central to arranging omiai, once a couple starts dating, they take a more hands-off approach, while still being available to provide advice to their clients and to check in with them about how their relationship is progressing. If all goes well, after about three months, the couple should be ready to get engaged, pay the seikonryō, and end the contract with their matchmakers.[11] Otherwise, the matchmakers will negotiate the breakup on their behalf, once one of the clients expresses a wish to put an end to things. In this case, both clients go back to the browsing stage once more, and set up more omiai with more potential spouses. Matchmakers must learn to guide clients through each of these stages, from informational first meetings with clients, through the omiai, onto deciding whether or not to marry a dating partner, and often enough, cheering them on to keep going after a breakup.

The hotel lobby, as mentioned above, is a working environment—one that I was initially invited to observe by Yasuda-sensei in the fall of 2009, after I met and interviewed her. Then, once I knew where the matchmakers worked, in a convenient public space, I made a point to go back on as many weekends as possible, visiting both the same hotel where I had originally met her, as well as neighboring hotels in Osaka. I quickly learned that the hotel lobby is also an informal learning environment, structured by observation of others along with storytelling and gossip. This is in part because matchmakers might spend a great deal of time there. They may have a full dossier of clients to meet, one every half-hour or so, depending on how many omiai they have scheduled for any given work day. There may be many, since most omiai are scheduled for weekend afternoons, when white-collar workers are most free. As waves of clients move into the hotel for their introductions and out of the hotel lobby and into a café for their omiai, the matchmakers who already know each other turn to one another, gather in clusters, and very soon begin to tell stories of this client or that client, this omiai or that omiai, this couple or that couple, who broke up, or that other couple, who are now engaged—to their own happiness, and the matchmakers' benefit.

Matchmakers' gossip is, in some sense, small talk: unimportant chatter to pass the time between the more significant events of making clients feel welcome and calm, and conducting introductions. However, this belies its educational and regulatory functions. Clients' bad manners are a frequent topic of conversation—stories abound of men too cheap to pay for coffee, for example, or treat his date to cake. As I became part of the regular hotel crowd, standing there with a notebook in hand and a stash of IRB-approved recruitment flyers explaining what I was up to, I was often included in these gossip practices. Matchmakers who were participants in my research, like Sugawara-sensei, would often include explicitly didactic notes as part of these stories, as a way of initiating me into the profession. Thus I learned: men must pay the café bill, and men who try not to are suspect. (Women are not accountable for paying.) Omiai have strict dress codes—don't show up in athleisure. Dating longer than three months is likely to lead to breakups—this, and other bits of matchmakers' conventional wisdom. It is gossip about clients, and the judgments that matchmakers issue upon them, that reflect and establish matchmakers' behavioral standards for themselves and their clients. For new matchmakers (or researchers), this kind of talk discursively negotiates standards of appropriate omiai behavior for matchmakers and their clients, along with elucidating practical theories of how single dates or entire relationships go off the rails.

In addition to this kind of informal networking, norm-making, and training, matchmaking organizations provide a number of formal means for learning the profession. One of these is simply the fact that organizations have organizational bylaws, governing the ways that matchmakers can "legally" interact with each other. Violations of these bylaws can lead to fines or, in serious cases, expulsion from the organization. They both codify and promulgate minimum standards of behavior. Matchmaker organizations also can and do offer their own formal training initiatives. For the NNK, formal training initiatives can help recruit new matchmakers to the profession and the organization. One-day focused workshops (*shūchū kōza*), along with online courses, are available for people who are considering taking up matchmaking as a profession or a side-hustle.[12] The NNK also operates its own seal of quality (*maruteki māku*), offering classes and a qualifying exam in order for their members to be able to operate not just as a nakōdo (matchmaker), but as a *nakōdo-shi*: their own neologism, based on terms for other professions, denoting a *professional, skilled* matchmaker.

In addition to these formal classes, during most weeks the NNK operates monthly meetings for local matchmakers in Japan's major cities (Tokyo, Osaka, Nagoya, etc.). The meetings are held in the afternoon, but in the mornings, members can attend optional training sessions on how to guide clients through signup, omiai, and kōsai. Member matchmakers can visit these classes over and over again, chatting with each other and engaging in role play in order to practice counseling clients. During the afternoon meetings, the president of the NNK takes questions from matchmakers about individual situations that confuse them, either directly from the assembled crowd, or from his emails. He offers his own opinion on these particular cases, and matchmakers who are present are also free to voice their opinions, ask additional questions, and otherwise negotiate a consensus as to how to proceed. In so doing, member matchmakers are able to negotiate norms around edge cases that perhaps the bylaws don't adequately address, as well as legal and ethical standards of behavior in dealing with clients as business professionals, rather than as neighbors or community members. A particular dramatic instance of this occurred when two clients negotiated their own breakup, and neither of the matchmakers knew how to deal with this, because the NNK bylaws did not actually specify that matchmakers *must* mediate a breakup, in the same way that they specify that matchmakers *must* set up an omiai. Nakanishi-sensei has often lamented that older matchmakers may still be operating on a communal model like the one described by Dore, where nakōdo perceive themselves as having a larger moral obligation to the couple and a desire to assist in situations that go beyond the making of matches, when clients run into trouble, as sometimes happens, especially when breakups and hurt feelings may be involved. By contrast, he recommends that disagreements between clients that go beyond the scope of a matchmaker's appropriate expertise and area of influence be referred to the police or lawyers, as appropriate.

Matchmakers are not the only party in matchmaking interactions who require education. Given that matchmaking is a minority practice, clients often have to be convinced of the value of it. In fact, matchmakers often advertise to parents of single adults, rather than to potential clients directly, reckoning that concerned parents will offer to foot the bill for the matchmaker, and thus their children can be persuaded to enroll (Nakanishi Kiyomi 2012). Matchmakers have two tasks: convincing their clients (or their clients' parents) that they know what they are doing, and educating their clients on appropriate behavior so that these clients will be suitable to introduce to others, as well as generally content with the matchmaking experience. Clients can be convinced that matchmakers know what they're doing by virtue of following their advice and seeing that it works—but this can't happen unless clients trust their matchmakers enough to try their advice in the first place. So what underlies the matchmaker's authority?

Successful and experienced matchmakers have a clear record that they can point to. Such successful matchmakers may also post pictures of happy couples that they have matched in their offices, or blog happy emails received from newly engaged or married clients. (Or, these days, post them to social media.) This serves to some extent as advertising—

"look what happiness can be yours!" At the same time, every smiling face and word of praise from happily married clients reinforces the matchmaker's position as an expert. For newer matchmakers who *don't* have this kind of substantial history of success, membership in a match-maker association can help establish a professional image, as well as going through formal training courses (where they are available). At the December 2011 Osaka meeting of the NNK, Nakanishi Keiji discussed "Marriage Appreciation Certificates" (*seikon kanshajō*) to be handed out in the new year, to each matchmaker who had at least one client marry. They were meant to serve as an official acknowledgment that the matchmaker in question was a capable member in good standing of the profession, in order to help them encourage clients to sign up. As he said:

> When people who are hoping to get married think, "I wonder where I should sign up?" They're wondering about whether there are many clients, whether there are good clients or bad clients, of course there's lots of things, but ul-timately one of the biggest, most important supports is, "are people getting married here?" "Is this matchmaker making matches?" I think this question is pretty much the deciding factor in whether they sign up or not.

The certificates, then, are meant to help the matchmaker sway potential clients' decisions in their favor, by testifying that, indeed, they have helped (at least one) couple(s) get married in the past.

Fujii-sensei, who used to give morning training lectures with the NNK that I attended in 2010, advised new matchmakers that they have to cre-ate a sort of character that incorporates their existing expertise. Similarly, at a workshop for inexperienced matchmakers in July 2012, the instructor encouraged new matchmakers to leverage their past careers as well as personal and professional connections, both for the purpose of attract-ing new clients, and also for establishing their expertise. For example, doctors or lawyers are already trusted professionals who could easily offer matchmaking services from their extant offices. Likewise, for those already employed in some other aspect of the marriage industry, or in re-lated industries (for example, jewelers), there is a natural logic to expand-ing into matchmaking, as well as a certain amount of expertise that carries over. Housewives, although they might lack business connections, can leverage their own happy marriages to establish their authority as new matchmakers. Moreover, as mentioned earlier, new matchmakers may also be able to sign on with more experienced colleagues and work as as-sistants, taking on an overflow of clients. In this way, they can gain their own experience while working under a name that already inspires trust.

Having established that the matchmaker is someone who can and should be trusted and listened to, client education begins with that first, in-person meeting between matchmaker and potential client, before the client decides whether to sign a contract with that matchmaker. During this meeting, the matchmaker explains the contract that the clients will sign. This contract primarily stipulates the fees that are due to the match-maker, which may include a sign-up fee (*nyūkaihi*), a monthly member-ship fee (*tsukikaihi*), a fee for each omiai (*omiairyō*), and, in the event of an engagement, the successful marriage fee (*seikonryō*). The contract may also stipulate the clients' responsibilities for an omiai, for example, showing up in a timely fashion, and not canceling or rescheduling except within certain limits. The contract, like organizational bylaws for the matchmak-ers themselves, is educational insofar as it dictates the minimum terms of acceptable behavior for clients, and the minimum obligations of the client to the matchmaker, and vice versa—for example, it may outline penalties for violating some of the rules of appropriate, polite, and decent behavior described above, such as fees to be assessed for lateness or cancelation.

The matchmaker may also begin the process of educating prospective clients on their relative value on the marriage market at their first meet-ing, before allowing them to sign up. Within the system of value created by the matchmakers, which places a high premium on finding individuals who can lead a comfortable, stable married life, not all clients are equally desirable. Matchmakers work with an incredibly heteronormative ideal of marriage, where children are meant to be an outcome of the relationship, husbands are generally breadwinners with solid employment, and wives are generally younger than their husbands, and planning to take at least some time away from work while their children are young. Because they don't fit comfortably into this heteronormative model, some would-be clients, due to age, looks, body type, income, family circumstances, ill-ness, or some combination of the above, will be treated by matchmakers, and potentially by other clients, as having a lower market value, or a decreased likelihood of getting married. A good personality may mitigate some of this, but certainly not all.

Matchmakers talk about this gendered state of affairs in an impression-istic, but empirical sense. These heteronormative views aren't necessarily their own beliefs about how marriage *should be*, but a common-sense ac-ceptance of how things simply *are*, as they see it. They portray women as having a tendency to choose men with elite educational backgrounds and high incomes, with a strong preference toward professionals such as doc-tors and lawyers. By contrast, they understand men's choices in potential partners to be based on women's youth and beauty. My experience is that matchmakers present these valuations straightforwardly when exchang-ing profiles or educating new matchmakers. For example, consider this blog post by Yamada Yumiko, from 2012. In it, she aims to both advise current clients and explain how matchmaking works to prospective clients. It is quite bald in its assessment of how much youth is exchangeable for how much income, and vice-versa:

★For the Ladies . . .
In your twenties, aim for the same age–10 years older
In your thirties, aim for 2–12 years older
★At this point, if your partner is 5 years older, choosing [someone] older gets the salary you want.

When you turn 38, 5–15 years older
When you turn 45, 5–20 years older
★At this point, if your partner is at least 10 years older, [someone] older will have a salary with wiggle room.

★As for the guys . . . I wrote about men's salaries on June 6th, but this time it's what men choose.

Just as women around 40 hurt when they're told that it's pointless to go for someone the same age, the age of women [you can apply to meet] changes with a guy's salary.

Guys
If you're in the range of 3 million yen, someone your own age.
Around 5 million yen, 3–5 years younger.
Around 8 million yen, 5–8 years younger.
If you've got 10 million yen, I think it'll be easy to get an OK from women 8–15 years younger.

Also . . . if you work someplace really famous, or you're amazingly good-looking, or you have a staggering educational background, you can aim 2–3 years younger, maybe~♪

Well, anyway, it's OK to apply!
(Yamada 2012)

Reading this is a bit appalling, but that is part of the point. As a result of clients' uneven market values, some will, as a matter of matchmakers' experiences, receive a disproportionate number of requests for omiai, while others—for example, highly educated women, or men with low incomes or educational achievement—may be comparatively difficult to marry off.[13] At the first training session for new matchmakers that I attended, led by Nakanishi Keiji-sensei, he cautioned his students against the temptation to flatter potential clients rather than educate them from the beginning about any of their personal disadvantages. He argues that flattery is ultimately bad business, and may result in disappointed, disillusioned, and dissatisfied clients. The matchmaker's job is to build trust and educate clients from the very beginning by speaking the truth about their realistic chances to marry, even when the truth is often harsh, misogynistic, and heteronormative. At the same time, as I suggest both here and in previous writing (Alpert 2014), the emphasis on conversational equality in matchmaking may, in some ways, model less heteronormative and more egalitarian modes of interacting for their clients.

Once a client has decided to sign up, further education, particularly education about self-presentation, may begin as clients put together their profiles and are introduced to the database where they can begin searching for members of the opposite sex to meet. It begins with selecting a photograph for the client's profile (if possible, professionally taken), and filling in basic information as described earlier. There may also be some delicate tweaking of the few areas of the profile that may be freely filled in by the client, in particular, the section on hobbies or interests. In early 2013, I attended a morning lesson held by Nakanishi Kiyomi on the art of profile writing, where she discussed the importance of this field at length. Hobbies on men's profiles that seem excessively solitary (fishing, video games), or for women, hobbies that seem potentially expensive (shopping, foreign travel) may scare off potential mates. According to her, the ultimate goal is to create a profile for someone who appears cooperative and other-oriented, rather than that of someone who seems solitary or selfish. Through setting up an appealing profile, matchmakers have their first opportunity to encourage clients to lean on them, to follow their advice. Even more than the possibility of meeting new people, advice on attitude and self-presentation is really what clients are paying their matchmakers for.

And, advice on self-presentation is precisely what clients get. In the process of arranging omiai, matchmakers counsel their clients on questions of how to dress and how to converse. Taking profile pictures, whether done by matchmakers, clients themselves, or by photo studios recommended to the client, provides an opportunity to create a visual representation of the omiai self—how to dress, style hair, do makeup. Some of the photo studios that the NNK worked with even offered pre-omiai services in order to style the client as in their profile photo.[14] Many matchmakers that I interviewed also discussed the issue of conversation, noting that male clients in particular suffered from a lack of knowing what to say or do during the conversation-intense encounter that is the modern, coffee-date omiai, where potential marriage partners have very little to focus on apart from each other. They suggested a number of remedial techniques for the conversation-impaired, such as moving dates to locations with activities built in, like shopping, or brushing up on local events with magazines so as to have ready topics of conversation at hand (Alpert 2014, 208–209).

Nakanishi Kiyomi's morning study sessions for matchmakers have also given me substantial insight into how matchmakers learn to counsel clients during the kōsai phase. In the several sessions I've attended over the last few years, I've had the opportunity to watch groups of around 20–25 matchmakers role play with each other as matchmaker and "client," in order to practice giving advice, and to share the situations they roleplayed and their imagined advice with their colleagues, for comment. Both Nakanishi-sensei's advice, and that of the participating matchmakers, tended to focus explicitly on "communication," and failures in it, as one of the primary reasons that relationships between clients fall apart instead of proceeding successfully along toward marriage. During kōsai, matchmakers push their clients to meet up with their new dating partners as frequently as possible (at least once a week over the course of three months is an ideal pace). But they will also continually act to make sure that the clients are communicating their intentions to marry each other, by texting each other regularly and discussing their feelings openly when they meet in person. They also make sure that clients are communicating to each other in a way that matchmakers believe is overt and intelligible. Both male and female clients may be under the mistaken assumption that the way they communicate their affections for their partner is readily understandable by others—for example, by putting effort into planning a date. One of the matchmaker's tasks when counseling clients through the dating phase is to inform them that this is not the case, and to guide communication toward semiotic modes, particularly explicit verbal declarations of feelings, that they privilege as being more clear and more understandable than other kinds of potentially meaningful actions.

Matchmakers' prioritizing of verbal self-expression reflects common romantic ideologies in Japan, which fixate on utterances like "I love you," even while imaging such bold emotional speech to be foreign to Japanese sensibilities. Hence, Jennifer Robertson (1998) notes that the extravagant and swoon-worthy romances routinely depicted by the all-female Takarazuka theatre troupe take place in a preponderance of foreign settings, so that performers can declaim their love at full volume without it being weird. As reality comes to imitate art (or perhaps, as neoliberal sensibilities continue to emphasize individuality in Japan), Alexy (2020) charts how "the romance of independence" has come to replace more "dependent," or "connected" models of coupled intimacy in Japan, which has coincided with an insistence on saying "I love you" outside of a romantic, fairy-tale, occidental context. Matchmakers' beliefs about communication thus can be seen as microcosms of larger shifts in how explicit verbal declarations of love are increasingly considered the foundation of a healthy and happy marriage in Japan.

THE MEANING IN THE MATCHES

Finally, I turn to the meaning that matchmakers find in their jobs, and the success—or lack thereof—of the matchmaking endeavor as a larger social project (to the extent that it can be imagined as such). The NNK advertises to potential matchmakers almost as much as they advertise to potential clients. In this advertising, they present matchmaking as a job where workers can feel happy because they are helping to raise low birth rates, contribute to society, and of course, make individual couples happy. Yet few clients ever get married. According to my interview with Ozeki-sensei, the success rate of omiai across all clients is not high at all—she estimated a 5 percent success rate for the large omiai companies. Similarly, Nakanishi Keiji estimated a 5–6 percent success rate in January 2010. The NNK's homepage presently boasts of 657 couples married, as their most recent yearly total, which is 1,314 clients.[15] Given their cited registration figures of approximately ten thousand clients, this is still only a 13 percent success rate—more than double the estimates cited above, but still depressingly low. How then do matchmakers make sense of the successes of their work, and their value for both individuals and society? Moreover, how do they understand the much more routine *failures* of the work that they do? In part, the answer lies in the neoliberal culture of self-responsibility that encourages individuals to make the effort to forge new connections through practices like matchmaking, and applauds pro-actively seeking professional help, but puts the responsibility for failure solely on the shoulders of clients.

Many matchmakers describe themselves as liking to take care of others, to the point of making a virtual job out of it. Then, something pushes them over the edge such that they make an *actual* job out of it. This seems to hold true for Aiba-sensei, a successful rural matchmaker who spoke at the October 2012 NNK association meeting. She called herself a "volunteer" who was good at matching people. It was only when she realized that she had three weddings to attend in the same month for couples that she had introduced, and couldn't afford different dresses for each, that she decided she ought to be turning a profit on her apparent natural talent. It is also true of Inasawa-sensei, the former business executive. Prior to taking up matchmaking professionally, he had been asked to informally make matches in his capacity as a connected and respected older person. When he was ultimately laid off, he decided to turn to matchmaking as his primary profession. Others begin stories of their entry into matchmak-ing with tales of their own happy omiai marriages—which holds true for popular matchmakers and teachers Fujii-sensei and Yasuda-sensei. There are also a few matchmakers that I interviewed, like Ozeki-sensei and Sugawara-sensei, who work as matchmakers in their spare time. Ozeki-sensei, who was by profession a designer, told me that she worked as a matchmaker in part for supplementary income, and in part because she is simply a romantic. Sugawara-sensei has at times had many jobs, each of them contributing an important piece of income, and all of them generally allowing her to retain her independence.

The reasons that matchmakers give explicitly, when asked, speak to their professional personae as people people. Other factors, which are only sometimes explicitly acknowledged, may also contribute to the desirability of matchmaking as either full- or part-time labor. One such feature is the ease with which interactions with clients and promotional work can be unobtrusively incorporated into daily life, and mixed in with other activities. Since 2007, I have spent many pleasant afternoons and evenings with Kawakami-sensei and her husband and business partner Takamiya-sensei, who operate their marriage bureau out of a cozy apartment in central Kyoto. Modern technology enables them to merge life and work. Their computer is in their living/dining room, and they can easily take a moment out of whatever else they happen to be doing to check and see which of their clients is setting up omiai, or who has emailed or texted. This is, in fact, what they do, periodically turning to the computer or their phones during the course of dinner on any given night that I've spent there. Messages received over SMS or, these days, on LINE, can also readily be received and responded to anywhere, at any time, and they can often take or make quick phone calls too.

That said, matchmakers and their professional associations predate the ubiquity of internet access in Japan. One or two matchmakers that I encountered still kept their records on paper at the time of our initial interviews; in times past, all member matchmakers would receive new client profiles by post every month. Ishiguchi-sensei, a male matchmaker that I met through the small social matchmaking group, had an office on the rural edge of Kyoto that was absolutely full of stacks and stacks of paper covering every available surface. But this was a vanishing practice ten years ago, and is certainly even more rare now, if not wholly nonexistent. Matchmakers frequently promote their businesses through websites, blogs, and social networks. (A simple Google search was how I found a number of initial interviewees, even back in 2007.) The NNK has a Facebook page for the public to like and follow and, in 2012, they put together a group blog that all the member matchmakers could post on, using the popular Japanese blogging platform Ameba.[16] Around the same time, they added tutorials on effective blogging and use of social media to some of the monthly meetings. Since most interaction with clients takes place through emails, text messages, and phone calls, many matchmakers get a second phone to manage. Since 2009, the growing number and abilities of smartphones, netbooks, and now tablets have made it even easier for matchmakers to be constantly in touch with their clients, at home or otherwise.

The reliance on technologically mediated communication in matchmaking also means that the barriers to entry into the field are quite low—all one needs is a computer, a mobile phone, and a little bit of money to register with a matchmaker association, and many people have the first two anyway, for other reasons. An office is nice, for those who can afford one, but is not a requirement, and many matchmakers never set up offices at all. Most of my interviews have taken place in homes, hotels, and coffee shops. Matchmaking can therefore provide a low-cost, low-risk way to attempt a transition into self-employment. At our first interview, Fujii-sensei gave this as a secondary reason for her entry into matchmaking, and it is a goal she successfully accomplished by the time I left Japan in 2013. Some of the newer matchmakers that I met at training sessions in 2010 were certainly hoping to reach the same level of success. Just as it can be challenging to know the success rates of matchmakers, or their number of clients, it can also be difficult to know how many people attempt to join the profession, but quickly drop out. Just as the barrier to entry is low, the losses sustained by those who try out matchmaking and leave without investing much are fairly minor. Most of the matchmakers that I've maintained contact with over the years are successfully making a living and committed to the profession—obviously. For those that I have fallen out of touch with, I wonder if it is simply that they fell out of my orbit, or if they fell out of the profession too.

This brings us back to the issue of making sense of failure. Do successful matchmakers who make a living doing this work have a higher rate than 10 percent? Do they simply have more clients, and thus more money coming in overall, regardless of their success rates? I honestly do not know, although my guess would be the latter. Even so, the most successful matchmakers still fail most of the time. If much of the pleasure of the job is taking care of people, but most people cannot be adequately cared for in the terms that matchmaking provides, is it still a pleasure? Matchmakers tend to attribute failure *and* success alike to their clients, both in terms of client attitude and behavior. Ozeki-sensei recommended to me that women be *sunao*—a difficult-to-translate word with overtones of "honest," "sincere," "pliant," and "compliant." A sunao woman, rather than finding fault with potential matches, will try to find one good thing about everybody. Ishiguchi-sensei reported that "people who are sunao and properly listen to what I say [get married] faster." Nakao-sensei also offered "sunao" as the first trait of clients who successfully marry. The matchmaker is the pro; the client who can accept her advice will do well.

Accepting the matchmaker's advice also entails the ability to handle rejection and criticism with relative equanimity; omiai are not for the easily-wounded. Sugawara-sensei offered "doesn't give up" (*akiramenai*) as the first trait of a successful client, and noted that many will start out excited but, after a few applications for omiai, and a few rejections, become discouraged and assume they are *dame*: "no good," somehow inadequate, or at fault. Sugawara-sensei also emphasized to me that clients should remember, when rejected at any stage in the process, that rejection doesn't mean that either client is a bad or undesirable person in any objective way, but means merely that the pair were not suited to each other, a point that Nakao-sensei also made when we talked. It is important to be able to bounce back from rejection, always ready to try meeting someone new. Someone—anyone—who can keep applying to meet people, and keep meeting them, without giving up, even in the face of rejection, is likely to be successful with time. Nakanishi Kiyomi-sensei's morning lessons on giving advice to clients during the kōsai stage have also proven instructive in this regard. One thing I've found in these practice counseling sessions is that when their "clients" express uncertainty about their partners, the matchmakers almost never advise them to break up. Rather, they advise them to continue seeing each other, making sure that they and their partners are communicating adequately with each other, making their feelings, desires, needs, and fears clearly known, and simply asking their partners questions that may be eating them up inside about what their partner really feels or thinks, why they haven't met each other's parents yet, and so on. Only after exchanging as much information as possible with each other should clients consider a breakup.

Relatedly, another quality that leads to success is the ability to *ganbaru* ("persevere"), to keep applying to meet people, to keep participating in many omiai, and date a lot of people, no matter how many times one is rejected, until success is achieved. Fujii-sensei described one of the services she offers to her clients as inspiring in them the spirit of "*issho ni ganbarō*," "let's keep at it together," until the client is successfully married. Sugawara-sensei applies this to her post-omiai counseling, encouraging women to meet any omiai partner at least one more time, as long as the omiai "wasn't awful" (*iya de nakattara*). In our interview, Nakao-sensei discussed the example of a man in Tokyo who succeeded for many reasons, by her account, but in part because he kept applying relentlessly to meet new women. Although she does most of her counseling over email and text message, she also said that she calls clients who aren't applying to meet new people into her office to suggest potential matches directly, which usually results in at least one or two omiai—progress. The more people their clients meet, as a matter of sheer mathematics, the more likely they are to meet someone that suits them. Yasuda-sensei and Fujii-sensei, the two matchmakers who made much of their own omiai marriages, both divulged specific numbers: the former participated in fifty-seven omiai before meeting her husband, and the latter, eighty-three. Underlying the ability to persevere is a certain kind of solid, constant self-assertion and proactiveness. If one desires to marry, one must actively seek marriage. It is not enough to want something; the desire must be a spur to continuous action in order to effect any kind of meaningful change.

This brings us back to the discourse of "self-responsibility" discussed earlier. In the face of structural barriers to marriage, or employment, the solution is not structural change, but rather, increased individual action, and increased individual responsibility for what does or doesn't happen in their lives. Clients who don't get married are either disadvantaged by their low market values, didn't listen to their matchmaker, or didn't try hard enough. Of course, the same discourse applies to matchmakers, and whether they succeed at this kind of entrepreneurial, independent work. If neoliberal subjectivity is based on managing the self as a business, then matchmakers, as individuals whose jobs and work "characters" are based on their experiences and innate personal qualities, are perhaps the ultimate neoliberal subjects. And yet, the matchmakers I've known, especially those I've known well, have truly all been kind people who I sincerely believe are doing their best within a profoundly imperfect system in Japan.

NOTES

1. Figures for more recent surveys were not available at the time of this writing.
2. Ironically, Faier's work documents how the term o-yome-san is used in relation to Filipina women who now often fulfill that role, supporting and perpetuating rural Japanese *ie* in their marriages to Japanese men.
3. To be fair, she was married before I moved away from Japan in 2013!
4. https://onet.co.jp
5. https://www.ibjapan.com/
6. https://www.omiaink.com/gaiyou. Data more current than 2018 is not available.
7. A quick look at the NNK's homepage shows that the limits have increased a bit since I did my fieldwork: https://www.omiaink.com/price
8. In the past, both men and women could easily serve as matchmakers, by virtue of either community connections or professional connections. In this ethnography, a number of male matchmakers figure prominently, either because they headed organizations, or because they were active parts of my social world. However, while I don't have exact figures, men are a decided minority in the field as it stands now, comprising perhaps one in every three to five matchmakers.
9. For more details on what these profiles actually look like, please see Alpert 2019.
10. In addition to the services that are beginning to cater to people who aren't looking for a heterosexual match, exceptions may also be made for *jijitsukon*, a "de

facto marriage," or cohabitation. This might be invoked in cases such as those of elderly couples where one partner might not be able to legally remarry without losing pension benefits from a previous spouse. In this case, the seikonryō is due to their matchmakers upon moving in together. It is thus not the case that matchmakers believe themselves strictly beholden to the letter of the heterosexual law, which makes the persistent heteronormativity of the industry a little bit more mysterious.

11. The dating period can generally be extended another three months, to six months total, but matchmakers are frequently wary of such indecision.

12. https://www.omiaink.com/business

13. The romantic problems faced by educated women are well-known and substantial. In the Japanese case, Raymo and Iwasawa (2005) discuss educated women's problems with reference to the concept of female hypergamy—the widespread idea in many societies that women must marry either a social equal or, even better a superior. (Men, meanwhile, are free to "marry down.") Women with increased educational attainment can earn enough to be independent from men, but their high achievements restrict their potential pool of socially appropriate partners to the small number of men who are as educated or as high-earning as they are. High-earning or highly educated men, meanwhile, are not similarly restricted and do not have the same incentive to choose high-earning or highly educated women in return.

The same logic applies in reverse to men with lower educational attainment or income. Just as having high education or income opens up the world of appropriate and interested partners for men, low income or educational accomplishment will restrict it, because the pressure on men to earn enough to singlehandedly sustain a family makes it embarrassing and emasculating for them to marry women with greater earning power. As mentioned in chapter 1, Emma Cook's study of marriage attitudes among casual laborers known as "freeters" (2014) reveals the prevalence of this ideology among men, even though statistical studies indicate that Japan is increasingly moving toward dual-earner households (Fukuda 2013).

14. See especially Alpert 2019.

15. https://www.omiaink.com/

16. The group blog now appears to be defunct, although many matchmakers belonging to the NNK maintain individual blogs.

.

4

✝

The Protean
Landscape of the Internet

Online dating has been slow to take hold in Japan, although it has become both popular and normalized in much of the West. Early on in my research with matchmakers, in 2007–2008, most Japanese people that I encountered regarded dating sites—more accurately, "meeting sites" (*deai-kei saito*)—with extreme suspicion. "Deai" simply means "meeting" or "encounter." While individual matchmakers and large marriage information services also promise their clients "deai" with new potential spouses, the word can also have strong sexual and illicit connotations. When I was a grad student in the mid–late 2000s, I was far too busy to meet anyone outside my department (or in fact, anyone I didn't run into in the course of the day, or share a class with). But there was a ready solution to my social malaise. Using popular sites like OKCupid and Match .com was, at the time, a common and generally unstigmatized practice among people around me in the midwestern United States, and I used them too, in the hopes of occasionally seeing humans outside my limited social set. (And I did. As one might predict, some of those encounters went better than others, but at least one led to a fifteen-year friendship, and that must surely be accounted a success of some kind.)

When I moved to Japan in 2008, in my mid-twenties and single, it was frankly depressing to open up OKCupid and realize how utterly useless it had become—but I wasn't really surprised. Looking for information on online dating in Japan during the same period, when I was conducting preliminary research, lead me to quickly realize that Japanese understandings of this practice were dramatically different to my own. One spectacularly over-the-top page from the Kyoto Prefectural Police has

stuck with me ever since I found it. The page presents striking cartoon il-
lustrations of shadowy sexual predators lurking behind an innocent-look-
ing schoolgirl who does not know what dangers await her as she looks at
her mobile phone, presumably at a deai-kei website. It then lists the potential dangers of these sites, as well as past criminal incidents associated
with dating site use (Kyoto Prefectural Police n.d.). The dangers it warns
of now seem decidedly outdated, although the page remained online
through 2019.[1] The first point in its case against dating sites is, "Neither
know the other's face or character." In this age of selfie-populated Tinder
profiles that are linked to Facebook and Instagram, the danger of not
knowing someone's face or character from their online presence seems
frankly laughable. At any rate, video chat through services like LINE—or
sometimes within dating apps themselves—would allow anyone to easily
check someone else out before meeting, and confirm that they are who
they claim to be in the profile. In fact, one happily married woman that I
interviewed in the summer of 2019, Emi, wouldn't have described herself
as having dated online. Nevertheless, she credited the internet with the
possibility of her marriage. She read something that her now-husband
had written online, and started corresponding with him over LINE. Texts
turned to video chat, video chat turned to an understanding, and that
understanding turned into a marriage.

Despite stories like Emi's, and the expansion of online dating in Japan
that characterized the 2010s, in some quarters, online dating retains its
sleazy reputation. Although Emi ultimately met her husband online,
she also told me that she had nearly signed up for online dating sites a
couple of times, lured by the ads, even entering in all her information.
However, she never wound up clicking the button to register because she
was nervous about spending money on what seemed to her like such an
unknown quantity. In July 2018, in his regular speech at the Osaka NNK
member's meeting, president Nakanishi Keiji bemoaned the growing
popularity of "deai-kei services" (his term), compared to the low numbers
of people signed up with matchmakers, despite the internet's dangers.
Attempting to discuss this very book with my old friend Takamiya-sensei
invariably results in similar comments about the (lack of) safety of online
services. On the one hand, I do believe matchmakers to be quite sincerely
concerned for the safety of their clients. But on the other, they also have a
professional interest in making sure online partner introduction systems
remain marginal to their own practices.

Based on my interviews with people who've used online matching
services, however, matchmakers might not have much to worry about.
Many of my interviewees employed multimodal strategies for searching
for partners, registering with online services *and* more traditional matchmaking options. While chatting with my recently married friend Seiko in

the summer of 2018 about her experience putting together a profile on a konkatsu site a few years previously, she maintained that the websites and the marriage bureaus she used were much the same in terms of the experience they offered. The difference, for her, was that the quality of people from the marriage bureau was higher. Another woman that I had interviewed the previous week, Misato, said that while online services were more fun (she used the very popular Japanese app "Pairs"), her marriage bureau was more effective because the quality of the clients was higher, and the bureau was what ultimately introduced her to her husband. And one week prior to *that*, an old acquaintance from Kawasaki, Masako, told me that she used the Yahoo Omiai service at the same time that she was attending omiai parties offline. Unlike the other two women, Masako didn't have much of a preference about offline versus online services. Ultimately, she regarded it as chance that she happened to meet her husband through Yahoo Omiai instead of one of the parties.

What the stories of these three women suggest is that Japanese singles tend to evaluate services based on the practical experience of using them and the results they get (or don't), rather than based on any kind of principled approach to the inherent safety or efficacy of one particular partner matching method or medium. In this chapter, I take up some of the changing ideas about the internet in Japan that have led to the growing popularity and acceptance of online partner matching services—even though many individuals can be reluctant to admit their participation in online dating, or, when asked how they met their partners, might elide the fact that they met online. The shifting landscape of social media in Japan has seen normalization and increasing popularity of international platforms like Facebook and Instagram over domestically produced sites like Mixi. These shifts have then led more Japanese to become more comfortable putting personal information such as their real names and pictures of themselves online. This is striking compared to Japan's local internet past, where usage tended to be pseudonymous and guarded. But the concept of konkatsu, brand new when I began my primary fieldwork, is now over a decade old. Instead of a fad, it's become an obvious thing for people to do if they want to get married. And the internet provides a potentially inexpensive alternative to matchmaking services, where fees can run into the thousands of dollars.

In addition to addressing their rising popularity, this chapter also attempts to map out the terrain of online matching services. Much as the previous chapter explored variations in neotraditional partner introduction services, with a focus on individual matchmakers, this chapter looks at the variety of websites available, the audiences they target, and the new language that has developed for discussing online dating in less stigmatized terms than "deai." It also looks at the role of language within the

sites itself—how language functions phatically online to create connections between people and how this differs from the kind of phatic labor
that matchmakers engage in. In conclusion, I argue that the line between
online and offline is blurry and slippery. Both services that bill themselves
as "online," as well as traditional "offline" matchmakers, cross in various
ways. What seems to matter more to *users* is the structure of the experience—not the extent to which it nominally happens online or otherwise.
Moreover, the world of matchmaking is aimed primarily at heterosexual
marriage, is attached to a particular kind of invented tradition, and has a
certain kind of respectable, trustworthy reputation to uphold, but online
venues have none of these restrictions. In exploring the landscape of these
apps, we can see growing egalitarianism in language, new visions of heterosexual relationships and of course, app services for those who aren't
heterosexual at all, in both domestic and international models.

NAVIGATING THE VIRTUAL
AND ACTUAL GEOGRAPHY OF APPLAND

There are a number of theories about what has made online dating more
palatable to Japanese users when—historically—the conventions of the
Western World Wide Web seemed suspicious to a Japanese audience.
A common example is the early success of the Japanese domestic social
network Mixi, which thrived for years while Facebook failed to break
into the Japanese market until the early 2010s. Both sites have similar
premises: replicating a person's offline social networks online. Both were
founded in 2004.[2] A key difference between them? Facebook's policy of
real names and real faces in profile photos, which was tremendously
off-putting in the Japanese context. While users put up real pictures of
themselves on Facebook (as required), researchers have found that people
who use both platforms have lower amounts of self-disclosure *and* higher
commitment to the platform on Mixi (Thomson and Ito 2012). Another
example is one of Japan's most famous and enduring contributions to the
worldwide internet: *Futaba Channeru* (two-leaf channel, 2chan for short)—
provided the template for 4chan and its legion of anonymous posters
(Coleman 2014, chapter 1). 2chan requires no registration, no avatars, and
no names. Perhaps most famously, it hosted the 2004 thread that became
the book (Nakano 2004), spin-off movie, and tv series called (in all cases)
Train Man (Densha Otoko), based on the optional, pseudonymous handle
of the main poster whose story it tells. While the story is based on a real
online *thread*, no one actually knows if the story itself is real, in the sense
of having actually happened to a person who could be identified as the

originator of the thread. The author of the book is given only as *Nakano Hitori*, "The Nakano Single."

Given this background, it is not surprising that some observers of the internet in Japan tie the rise of online dating to growing acceptance of Facebook and concomitant acceptance of putting real-life information online for broad-based consumption, in line with Facebook's policies. No one seems to be entirely sure what changed, exactly, but commentaters tend to point to the period around 2011–2012 as a significant turning point. Gilhooley (2012) cites a number of possible factors that could have contributed to the shift in social network usage, ranging from the simplicity and freedom of Facebook's interface to its practical value for coordinating relief efforts after the Great East Japan Earthquake in March 2011. For example, using real names allowed Facebook users to help identify and search for the missing. Educators have suggested that Facebook is useful for teaching and learning English because of the different language options for the interface and its ability to function "as a platform for a link to the world" (Hamada 2012, 104), connecting Japanese English learners with English speakers from all over. Finally, and *also* in 2012, a new app within the Facebook interface called "Omiai" appeared out of nowhere, but then was suddenly everywhere (Miyamoto and Seo 2012). Perhaps Facebook, with its networks of people connected by real-world ties to each other, with real names that could be held accountable for misbehavior, seemed more like a matchmaker's database than a deai-kei site, just waiting for a platform-specific app to take advantage of it. The name, "Omiai," also probably did a lot of heavy lifting in the service of reframing online dating. By naming itself after the traditional first meeting of potential spouses in Japanese matchmaking practices, Omiai implicitly proposed to Japanese internet users that the internet could broker your relationships just as safely as matchmakers of old—and like matchmakers, widen your circle of acquaintances. It still seems to be going strong, and has since spun off into an independent app.

Of course, various kinds of dating and partner matching sites clearly existed before Omiai. So did the concept of *netto* ("net," online) *omiai*. However, the Omiai Facebook app may have served as a useful proof of concept for the online dating industry, and seemed to take off in a way that previous sites and apps had not. Now, a variety of locally produced websites and apps, catering to local sensibilities, continue to borrow the language of matchmaking and characterize their services as omiai, the formal introductions provided by matchmakers. Some foreign sites, like Match.com, have also localized themselves using the language of konkatsu and adopted local practices like uploading proof of identity to the site to ensure safe encounters online. And, despite the lack of broad legal recognition of same-sex relationships in Japan, net omiai and konkatsu have even expanded into the gay male dating market, with services like Bridge offering both a konkatsu app as well as in-person counseling at a location in west Shinjuku, Tokyo.[3] Another service, Resally, supports both gay men and lesbians in their search for "serious encounters" (*majime na deai*), and offers both an app and in-person omiai parties, with physical locations in Tokyo and Osaka and events around the country.[4]

But not all apps are quite so serious, and the linguistic relationship goes both ways. Konkatsu has restructured the world of online dating, but the world of dating apps has, in return, revised some of the language of konkatsu. I left Japan in 2013 to finish and defend my dissertation. When I returned to Japan for a research trip two years later, in the summer of 2015, the word *koikatsu* had suddenly sprouted everywhere, a speciation event in the specific vocabulary of dating in Japan. "Koikatsu" replaces the "marriage" part of "marriage activities"—the character 婚—with the character 恋, meaning (romantic) love. Ergo: koikatsu ("love hunting"), by analogy with konkatsu ("marriage hunting"), by analogy with shūkatsu ("job hunting"). Moreover, in 2015, the term was new enough that I could have a debate with a grad student friend over how it was supposed to be pronounced, since Japanese kanji can often be read multiple ways.[5] On that research trip, one of my goals was to gather information from companies themselves about their products. As I learned from an interview with a representative of Diverse Inc., which produces multiple konkatsu and koikatsu platforms, terms like "koikatsu" are deliberate industry creations meant to move away from the sleazy language of deai to suggest that searching for love or dating online needn't be shameful.

The variety of partner matching platforms produced domestically are likewise aimed at a variety of groups, who desire a variety of different relationships. Online omiai and konkatsu sites target roughly the same group of consumers as matchmakers—perhaps a more budget-conscious group of them, since online-only platforms are often cheaper. They may also target a more reticent group who shy away from the effervescent sociality of matchmakers, even though the online platforms require such shy individuals to do all of their own phatic labor. Koikatsu sites and apps target those who might look to "online dating" in another cultural and linguistic context. And, of course, the hookup apps, the deai-kei world, still exists. My friend Marie, a formerly avid user of Tinder, that leviathan of the online dating world, sometimes characterized it as "really" deai-kei. In Japanese, Tinder.com bills the app as the "world's most wide-spread lifestyle app" (*sekai saidaikyū no raifusutairu apuri*). But when I swiped through profiles with Marie to see how she evaluated them, it revealed her deep concern with analyzing both pictures and text to identify and avoid men whose profiles hinted that they were already married and looking for an affair, or suggested an interest in only casual sex. While this implies that many users *were* looking for something more "honest," or something more "serious," it also suggests that *enough* users approach Tinder with a deai-kei frame of mind for it to be a concern for other users. But this is possible precisely because the world of "matching" sites and apps can, in general, be more flexible and playful than marriage bureaus, and can serve a wider array of interests.

To speak of Tinder is to speak of the influence of foreign social media systems on Japan's social media culture, perhaps in large part due to the rise of location-based dating apps that simply find and display users nearby in lieu of a search function. This has been dramatic to witness during the years I've spent in Kazakhstan, in a way that also illustrates some of what has likely happened in Japan[6]—especially since, when I moved to Kazakhstan, I was (still) single and curious myself about how I might meet people. To the best of my knowledge, Kazakhstan has little extant online dating culture. Additionally, Cynthia Werner notes that Soviet law outlawed most practices related to arranged marriages, and few have attempted to revive them (2009, 319–321). That is to say, neither of the frameworks through which many people around the world make sense of online dating—newspaper personals or matchmaking online—are especially salient here. And yet, since moving here in 2014, I have observed that the population using Tinder in urban Kazakhstan has grown and grown. In 2015, it was possible to quickly swipe to the end of Tinder in Astana, and most of the people I saw using it were not local—they tended to be North American, Middle Eastern, or European migrants, or travelers just passing through.[7] Now there is a substantially larger number of users on the app. The persistent *can* still swipe through all of Astana Tinder, but it takes several hours. And while there are still plenty of migrants using Tinder, the growth is in profiles from locals who hear about the app and give it a try.

This example demonstrates that location-based apps have the potential to bring online dating wherever they go, even if there isn't an established culture of it.[8] The presence of travelers whose mobile phones already have the app installed means that from the beginning, there are other people to find using the platform. Apps like Tinder also provide a comfortable and familiar platform for migrants looking for love who may not be proficient in written or spoken Japanese; many of the locally produced apps have limited language options, if any at all apart from Japanese.[9] This travel is a two-way street. Just as visitors to Japan bring Tinder along, Japanese users may learn about or bring the app with *them* as they move abroad for work or study themselves, in a back and forth flow of cultural influence and exchange.[10]

How, then, do users navigate among the proliferation of available apps, and choose which ones they want to try? Interviews with online daters suggest that other users form a significant part of their evaluations of the platforms they tried, in terms of both user quantity and quality. Tinder attracted a fair number of my interviewees, in part because some preferred its international style, but also in part because Tinder just has *so many people* using it. For my friend Ryan, who had moved to Tokyo after some years living in a relatively rural area, the greater number of people in Japan's largest urban center—and the greater number of people on Tinder specifically—meant there was eternal cause for hope. Ryan said that in the countryside, he just had to meet everybody he found, because there were so few people (specifically gay men) to be found in the first place. In Tokyo, he could be choosy. I also had a chance to meet a bicultural straight couple in Tokyo, Catherine and Masa. Both of them were people whose lives, heritage, and families had been split between Japan and the United States. Both told me that they came a little late to Tinder, but loved it for the simplicity of the interface and the sheer volume of other users, which made meeting people easy. Prior to their relationship, Catherine mentioned meeting up with other users regularly, incorporating interactions with her matches into her social life at concerts and clubs in Tokyo.

As the above suggests, popularity is a major criterion for choosing an app, either in a broad sense of the raw number of users an app has, or among friends making recommendations to each other. The case of Mika, who used Tinder with her friends as a form of communal entertainment, suggests one way that friends might recommend matching services to each other: by getting their phones out, showing each other how they're used in person, and having fun together. This was dramatized for me during my first summer of interviews in 2018 by two new friends, Arisa and Hanako. Arisa used Tinder extensively for entertainment, carrying on long conversations with men that she only rarely, if ever, met in person. Over dinner, I watched her convince Hanako to give it a try by telling stories that were probably even more entertaining than the actual conversations. The next year, when I caught up with them, Hanako reported that she had indeed tried Tinder, although she quickly abandoned it, deeming herself a failure. Arisa, meanwhile, had grown somewhat disillusioned with Tinder, and promoted the virtues of Bumble instead. She said that Bumble users were more serious, and didn't hide their faces in their profiles—a striking contrast to other platforms where Arisa lamented the fact that everyone *claims* to be honest, but isn't. Other apps that have come up in the course of my discussions with interviewees included Badoo, Happn, Tapple, and Pairs. All of these were apps that my interviewees tried because they were recommended to them—and when I next see Hanako, I wonder if she'll have given Bumble a try.[11]

In addition to getting recommendations from friends, users look to the audience of the site to see if it suits their personal goals. Seiko, Misato, and Masako all specifically wanted to get married, so they looked for sites specifically designed for konkatsu, or with an emphasis on it, like Pairs and Yahoo Omiai. Others, with less specific goals, were more willing to try more amorphous apps that welcomed people searching for a variety of different relationship types. Above and beyond just having a substantial user base, people trying out online partner matching services also looked to the *quality* of that user base. Most of the users I interviewed were looking for, in some way or another, users who seemed *normal*, who seemed safe, and who seemed serious. Misato tried Pairs because it had lots of users and, since it was a local app, meshed with her sensibilities. However, she eventually gave up on Pairs after two years and twenty first dates—she never had a second one with anyone she met through the app, in part because she didn't want to see any of them again. For her, this pointed to the comparative value of her marriage bureau, which was introducing her to people she *did* want to see again. Another woman engaged in konkatsu, Kaori, specifically chose a site that requires users to pay in order to be active (Zexy Enmusubi), in order to ensure that everyone using it was at least serious enough about wanting to get married to pay ¥2,400 per month.[12] App choice is also not static. Some users may try out multiple sites to get a feel for the interface and the users, and later pick one or two to invest time in and check regularly, abandoning their profiles on the rest. They may also switch platforms or even entire strategies over time if they become frustrated or disappointed, like Arisa or Misato.

Additionally, like Kaori, online daters in Japan may look to either app affordances or barriers to entry, like a paywall, that they see as encouraging serious users, and improving the overall quality of the user base. An example is Arisa's switch to Bumble. Why would she claim that its users are more sincere, and why would Bumble be a good choice for users who are tired of Tinder? Both Bumble and Tinder are international, location-based matching apps, where users have to match before messages can be sent—so they have similar interfaces and operate according to similar matching logic. Bumble's more "serious" reputation may be because of its mechanism that requires women to send the first message in heterosexual pairings. Men using Bumble therefore have to evince a certain attractive patience, since they are not allowed to control the interaction from the beginning. Sincerity, on the one hand, is the condition of having internal thoughts that match external words or deeds, such that we can take those words "seriously" (Austin 1962, 9–10). However, it is also "speech . . . which is compelled by nothing that might lie 'outside' the speaker, whether that be . . . political authority, written texts, or social conventions" (Keane 2007, 214). By its very nature, "sincerity" or "seriousness" are invisible; as Keane notes, they require some kind of external performance to be socially legible. App users therefore require some sort of externally available semiotic proof—a sign—that points to a "sincere" mindset. For Kaori, willingness to spend money was that sign; for Arisa, the sign was the choice of app itself. Any man who signs up for Bumble is, in theory, publicly taking an egalitarian stance on communication in relationships.

CREATING PROFILES AND SEARCHING

Matchmaking services have relatively standard profiles and offer search options for all their databases. Users enter in their own desired criteria (perhaps an age range, or an income range, or a location), and from there, browse through the search results to see who they like. While there are thousands of kekkon sōdan-sho and perhaps dozens of umbrella organizations and databases, they aim to distinguish themselves from one another by their quality, their success rates, and by the personal character or charisma of the matchmakers or counselors who can inspire, comfort, and guide their clients. The style, routine, and system of matchmaking itself is fairly fixed by professional agreement among the community of matchmakers. It changes—obviously—but it changes slowly. By contrast, online options distinguish themselves based on their different profile styles, interfaces, and affordances for showing users to one another and allowing or encouraging them to interact. This means that profiles may vary wildly from platform to platform and may also vary wildly *within* a single platform as well. To some extent this depends on the amount of freedom each site allows users in filling out their profiles. Some fields are populated by preselected choices from drop-down menus; users can only pick from one of those choices or leave that field blank. By contrast, some fields may be free text fields, allowing the user to write whatever they want, within the character limit; a long character limit may encourage users to write more. We also have to consider which fields are mandatory for users to fill in, and which users are allowed to leave blank. In addition to these app structure constraints and affordances, platforms also vary in terms of what kinds of help, advice, and documentation they give to their users. The techniques of user profile creation thus vary substantially from app to app.

Another difference between matchmaking services and online matching apps is that users are fully in control of their own profiles, not just in terms of their creation, but also in terms of their maintenance. Users can update their profiles at any time, in any way, so long as they do so within the community guidelines of each platform and its technical affordances.

They can do so as they need, as the mood strikes them, or as they gain more experience with the platform and decide to alter their strategies for self-presentation. One of my favorite examples comes from Marie, who is a divorced single mother. Originally, she put "sexy" pictures of herself wearing makeup on her Tinder profile. These certainly attracted attention—but not really the kind she wanted. The sexy pictures, perhaps predictably, appealed to men who mainly wanted sex. By contrast, Marie wanted to be seen as a whole person and, for the sake of her son, wanted to date people who could be comfortable with her child. So, she changed her pictures to bare-faced shots that included her son in them. Eventually, she wound up in a long-term relationship with an Australian man who adores her son and wants to live as a family—someone that she thinks sees her as that whole person.

Profile construction is thus a dynamic activity that takes place in both the context of specific platforms and in the small-scale historical context of every individual user's experience, rather than a fixed kind of self-presentation. The friends who teach users about the existence of particular services may also give practical advice on usage and self-presentation strategies, as with Arisa and Hanako. One man that I interviewed, Kazuhito, was introduced to Tinder during his time living in Amsterdam; previously, living in Japan, he had favored offline strategies for meeting potential romantic partners. Even in Amsterdam, Tinder was never his only method for meeting potential partners—he also used language exchanges and drinking parties (*nomikai*) to introduce himself to new people. Because the newness and strangeness of Tinder made him feel embarrassed, he had a friend take a silly, fun picture of him. By contrast, Noriko, in her late thirties, approached online konkatsu and dating by seeking professional advice. She originally met with a consultant to develop a profile for Yahoo Omiai, which she used and later abandoned. When she tried again after a gap of a few years, she just reused the same profile, since, after all, it was good. During her second try, she did successfully meet someone and marry, using Pairs.

In addition to learning about profile construction experientially and experimentally, in dialogue with friends and with the reactions their profiles produce (or don't), users might turn to different types of documentation provided by the services that they use in order to figure out what to do and how to present themselves. Just as online matching services vary substantially in their design, they also vary substantially—of course—in the kinds of help documentation that they provide to users, based who they imagine their users are, and consequently, what kinds of assistance that these imagined users need. Tinder, for example, provides basic explanations and technical support for using the app, along with a blog about app updates.[13] Tinder's help documentation also includes substantial advice on safety. This includes an introduction to automated tools they use to keep the platform safe, and the reporting tools built into the app for users who engage in unpleasant, or worse, criminal behavior. They also have a page on "Tips and Tricks for Using [Tinder] Safely" (*Anzen ni Tsukau Tame no Kotsu*), which includes cautions about long distance and international romances, meeting dates in public places, the hazards of traveling for LGBTQ+ individuals, protecting oneself with condoms, and the importance of sexual consent.[14] These are all very practical and real concerns for anyone meeting people online, to be sure. However, the general lack of non-technical information about how to use the site suggests that Tinder imagines that the process of putting together a profile with pictures and text, sorting through profiles, or communicating with other users is self-evident and straightforward.

By contrast, Dalton and Dales (2016), in their survey of five konkatsu sites, note how common it is for the help documentation to guide users toward particular (gendered) patterns of site use by suggesting that women search for "doctors" and "business owners" and that men search for "nurses" or "teachers" (2016, 9). YouBride, one of the five sites they examine, has a user guide available publicly on their website.[15] In addition to teaching users about the functionality of the site, YouBride's guide also has advice on "how to take a good picture," suggests specifically uploading *two* pictures (one clearly showing the face, another with a pet or a hobby), and informs users that profiles with pictures attached get three times as many responses. Later, the guide gives tips for searching and sending messages to other users. (When writing a message, read the other person's profile carefully and focus on points in common!)

Another konkatsu site, Zexy Enmusubi, provides sample profile text during the profile editing process, for users who might not know what to write. In other words, these sites do *not* assume that the process of self-presentation or communication is transparent or something that users already know how to do without needing explicit instruction. Of course, YouBride and Zexy Enmusubi *also* provide information about basic safety when contacting and meeting strangers from the internet—although the sex advice is distinctly absent.[16] In general, it's fair to say that YouBride and Zexy Enmusubi have a rather different view of what kinds of advice and support their users might need—and provide radically different sets of help documentation, accordingly. Both of these are konkatsu apps, but other kinds of domestically produced matching apps also have similar documentation. Generally, Japanese apps assume that, in addition to encountering technical difficulties, their users may have absolutely no idea what they are doing, or what any of the fields in the profile are for, or how to fill them in.

Of course, the two paragraphs above also compare a famous international app with less widely-known, Japan-specific apps. This might be unfair. It is reasonable to assume that someone using a less widely known app might very well need additional guidance on how it functions. But it also points to the general *newness* of the enterprise of online partner matching in Japan. Presenting one's "real" self (more or less) online for ultimately offline ends has a relatively short history in Japan, while in North America, online dating sites are the heirs of a long history of newspaper personal ads that date back to the late seventeenth century. Historian H. G. Cocks (2010) provides a comprehensive history of personal ads in the British context, and notes in the very beginning that it only took about fifty years from the invention of the modern newspaper until the invention of the personal ad—and they have continued ever since. To the best of my knowledge, Japanese newspapers do not have this history.[17] In the absence of a long tradition of advertising personal romantic difficulties and desire in public fora, Japanese users of online dating sites lack existing cultural models for how one might use online partner matching services that deviate from the omiai or konkatsu model more closely modeled on historical and familiar Japanese practices.

THE PHATIC TECHNIQUES OF PROFILES

Having outlined the array of services out there and their varying appeals to different classes of imagined users, I now wish to turn to the question of the practical details of creating a profile, searching for users, evaluating other profiles, and initiating communication in some fashion or another, in order to examine the concrete phatic strategies employed by Japanese users of online matching services. It is somewhat inherently difficult to generalize about this, for reasons discussed directly above. Different online matching services present users to each other in different ways, using some combination of text and pictures, required fields and optional ones, empty text boxes, and drop-down menus with pre-selected options. The resulting assemblage—a profile—provides users with a way to strategically represent themselves to potential partners. It also serves as material with which that same user, while browsing, might begin to evaluate other users as potential partners, and decide whether to "like" them or send a message to attempt to begin a conversation. These profiles vary tremendously in length, both from one profile to another, and one site to another. They also vary in terms of the relative emphases they put on images versus text, the amount and kind of text they expect or encourage users to generate on their own, the amount of time they imagine users might spend contemplating others' profiles, and the ways they enable users' profiles to be searched or otherwise discovered.

Let us illustrate these difficulties with two concrete examples. At one end of a continuum from "free form" to "structure," we might consider Tinder. Tinder's interface contains large pictures, with minimal text superimposed over them at the bottom. It has a minimal number of fields that can be filled in: name, job, educational background, "about me." None of these fields, save the name, are mandatory—and the name doesn't have to be filled in with anything beyond a single letter. (Age is also mandatory for free users, but can be hidden with a paid account.) Up until very recently—early 2020—viewing the "about me" text generally required extra effort on the user's part—extra swipes and taps to reveal it, if it has been filled in at all. Now, if there is any text in this field, Tinder will serve up a limited preview superimposed on the bottom of the first picture. Extra taps are still required to view the whole text. But often, there isn't any text in this field at all to preview. An interface that deprioritizes text also disincentivizes users to produce any. In addition to its minimal profile requirements, user discovery on Tinder is similarly minimalist. The app serves up profiles one at a time, based on proximity to the user (with the help of GPS data), and other algorithmic considerations besides. In order to view the next profile, users must swipe either left to dismiss the current profile, or right to express interest in contacting the other user in front of them. Although users can set their preferences to narrow down which profiles they might be served based on gender, physical distance from each other, and age range, no search is possible.

At the other end, let us consider the konkatsu site Zexy Enmusubi. "En" means "destiny" or a fated "connection" between people, while "musubi" literally means "tying." It generally refers to the creation of marriage bonds, poetically, in the sense of two people binding their fates to each other. While Tinder places its pictures front and center, Zexy Enmusubi has a *wide* array of fields to fill in, and gives equal pride of place in the profile to information like name, age, hometown, current residence, height, body type, blood type, and birth order, under the rubric of "basic information" (*kihon jōhō*), which is but the first of six sections that can be filled in. For anyone who has ever taken a Japanese class, these typical elements of a self-introduction (*jiko shōkai*) will seem very familiar, and closely parallel the kinds of information someone might provide when introducing themself in person.[18] Only a fraction of these fields are mandatory, but even this fraction is substantially more than that required by Tinder. Unlike Tinder, Zexy Enmusubi has a search function, and users can search on any and all of the fields in the profile in order to find a marriage partner with, for example, the exact same preferences in married lifestyle, or similar (or different!) family backgrounds. We can readily imagine that Zexy Enmusubi users might approach the act of profile creation and evaluation very differently.

I have no wish to suggest that the design of technology determines how people will use it. As numerous writers on society and technology have noted, people will always build their own structures into, around, and on top of the structure of any technology they are given. Prior to the development of specific web platforms designed for partner matching, some Japanese singles used—and are still using—bulletin-board software to accomplish the same ends. Thomas Baudinette (2017) provides a detailed look at the language of recent gay bulletin board dating practices, and Ryan discussed using message boards before apps were ubiquitous in the gay community. At the same time, as Bonnie Nardi notes with regard to changes in the raiding structure in *World of Warcraft*, "design of a software artifact . . . may powerfully shape human activity" (2009, 68). In Nardi's example, guilds designed for larger raids fractured and disbanded after the introduction of content that favored smaller parties, as the new structure wound up leaving many people out of formerly large, communal, activities. Likewise, Nardi notes that software enforces rules automatically, without the negotiations made possible in systems operated by human decisions (62–63). In a similar fashion, online partner matching platforms have certain restrictions that cannot be overridden—fields that *must* be filled in before the user can move on to the next stage of profile creation or editing, for example. These restrictions, along with platform-specific social worlds shaped by technological design (searches vs. algorithmic geolocal discovery of profiles), will necessarily result in different individual and social approaches of users to particular platforms, and the design of the technology may even play a critical role in a user choosing that platform.

In other writing (Alpert 2019), I have discussed the question of strategies for both designing and selecting profile pictures in matchmaking and, to some extent, in more purely online services as well. Pictures are absolutely critical for profiles in all branches of the marriage industry, and profiles without them are indeed extremely unlikely to get responses. Matchmakers can photograph clients themselves as part of the intake process, and they commonly refer their clients to photo studios as well. Online platforms have to guide users to upload pictures as part of the profile creation process, and as discussed above in the example of You-Bride, may take the time to explain why pictures are necessary to increase the number of positive responses (matches, messages). Some sites, such as Zexy Enmusubi, provide the option to automatically exclude profiles without photos in search results, such that, in addition to their lack of phatic *appeal*, profiles without photos are also functionally limited in their phatic potential, given that they are less likely to ever even be seen by other users.

Other sites try to maximize the phatic appeal of profiles and their photos via algorithmic tricks or detailed user guides. Tinder's documentation, for example, introduces its "Smart Photo" functionality that will automatically prioritize and display first those photos that increase the likelihood of another user "liking" the profile. It also advises users that they need at least three pictures uploaded in order to use this feature.[19] The Pairs website provides information about what kinds of photos can enhance your profile—photos depicting your tastes or hobbies—and thus increase the rate of matches.[20] Here, we see the Japanese self-introduction logic at work again; it also operates on the gay men's app Nine Monsters (Alpert 2020). All of that said, my goal is to focus on profile *language* as a frequently under-appreciated but nonetheless critical aspect of the profile. Photos can be powerful draws, but my interview data suggests that written components of the profile can prove just as decisive for users in terms of whether or not they interact with a profile or summarily dismiss it.

Language is also relevant here because a social media profile—of which the dating site profile is a distinct subset—is a particular, recognized genre of writing, at least, in some societies and in some circumstances. Bauman (2000) defines genre with reference to intertextuality—texts or utterances are perceived as belonging to a specific genre because they reference other, similar texts. A set phrase like the "once upon a time" of a fairytale or the "single gentleman seeks partner in crime" of the increasingly antique newspaper personal ad "carries with it a set of expectations concerning the further unfolding of the the the discourse" (2000, 84). A text that does not conform to our expectations of the genre we expect to be reading can become unintelligible, or signal that its author is somehow abnormal by virtue of their inability or unwillingness to produce a profile that adheres to the conventions of the genre.

One of the issues with regard to producing online profiles in Japan, however, is the wobbly, uncertain, and new nature of the social media profile as a genre of Japanese popular writing, and the even newer nature of the online matching profile. In the Japanese context, online partner matching can be seen, at least in part, as a foreign import, without extant local models of self-advertisement from before the internet that can be remediated online. This stands in contrast to contexts like India, where matchmaking via newspaper ads has a substantial history from the twentieth century onward (Gist 1953). Agrawal notes that while online matchmaking portals facilitate traditional matchmaking for educated Indian urbanites, they also help kin collaborate at a distance when in-person social networks have become attenuated, and moreover, that "one of the attractions of these new services is its capacity to simultaneously address seemingly contradictory demands" (2015, 16). They do this by providing the opportunity for singles to write more about themselves in free text and narrow down searches for more specific personal preferences in a partner, and offering options that put companionate marriage norms at the forefront of their drop-down menu options (20). Consequently, marriage via online matchmaking blurs the boundaries between dichotomies like "arranged" and "love," or "traditional" and "transgressive."

But in comparison to India, again where practices of arranged marriage have changed but nonetheless remain strong, the rapid decline in the popularity of arranged marriages in Japan from the middle of the twentieth century onward seems to have been one obstacle to matchmaking following the Indian trajectory; differing attitudes about media and privacy, as we can see in the discussion of changing patterns of self-disclosure online, probably also played a role. Contemporary online partner matching services and their users in Japan are thus reinventing traditions for presenting users as potential spouses or lovers, but rather than an intertextual evocation of a newspaper ad, Japanese profiles invoke the conventions of the *tsurisho* ("fishing papers") of the nakōdo, the online dating profiles of international services developed mainly in the English-speaking world, and the evolving preferences and internet usage patterns of contemporary Japanese singles on local and international social media.[21]

So what does the genre-in-progress of an online profile look like? My interviewees were clearly able to point to some features, such as the pressure to adhere to particular conventions and the appearance of more-or-less fixed phrases across profiles, creating the intertextual network needed for generic formation. In chatting with Seiko about her experiences with both konkatsu sites and marriage bureaus, she found that profiles were very similar between the two services, and also very similar between users. In writing her own profile, she felt a strong pressure to conform—to not stick out too much, and to produce the kind of profile associated with a safe, marriageable person. Other users of konkatsu sites that I interviewed reported similar experiences. But this experience was not universal. Masako felt that "there are a lot of weird people like me online," and that the internet perhaps gave stranger strangers a better opportunity to find each other.

Interviewees using other services were also readily able to point to recognizable tropes in profile construction, to which they had attached particular interpretations. Mika, the social Tinder user, told me that if a man has filled in his university, but not his job, it means his job is probably unimpressive, but he went to a good school. Both Mika and Marie were also concerned with using profile text (and pictures, to some extent) to identify men who ought best to be avoided. Certain repeated phrases in men's profiles like "looking for friends to have a casual drink with" stood out to them as red flags indicating someone only looking for sex, perhaps because they're married and unable to have a more substantial relationship. Ryan, as a gay man on Tinder, shared with me some of the shorthand gay men have developed on the platform to share their sexual preferences with others who are in on the secret, but without the meaning being obvious to those who aren't. One example is using the Chinese characters for "convex" (凸) and "concave" (凹) as shorthand for "sexually interested in penetrating" and "sexually interested in being penetrated," respectively. All of these testimonies suggest that there is some predictability in how online daters go about assembling images and text into something that more or less recognizably fits into the genre of "profile," and moreover, identifies them as particular kinds of relationship seekers.

At the same time, my own qualitative analysis of user profiles from Japanese sites shows that, in the absence of clear documentation from sites, user profiles vary *substantially*, in ways that suggest clear genre conventions are a work in progress for user profiles on koikatsu and deai-kei platforms—although according to Seiko's experiences, konkatsu services, with their clearer links to omiai, seem to have a more recognizable and rigid style. Some of the variation in users' profiles also seems to be linked also to the cultural origin of the services and thus the variation in the kinds of documentation and guidance that they make available to their users. As discussed earlier, platforms designed in Japan provide a greater degree of explanation to users. This may be in part due to a more didactic sensibility that is part of the Japanese internet more generally, and in part due to the newness of online partner matching more specifically. On Zexy Enmusubi, user profiles seem fairly uniform, because the site itself provides sample text that instructs users in the implicit generic conventions of profile writing. I have not seen this level of detailed guidance in other sites I have examined, and part of what makes Zexy Enmusubi especially fascinating is precisely this deep affection for detail. Here is one of twelve sample profile options that will automatically populate the free text field for Zexy Enmusubi users with the click of a button:

こんばんは、初めまして！
●●出身、現在は●●に住んでいる××歳です。
仕事は◆◆関係です。

今までは仕事が忙しく、恋愛や結婚をあまり考えていませんでしたが、
最近真剣に結婚したい！と思えるようになり、
一緒に時間を共有できる人が出来たらいいなと思い、登録しました。

周りからはよく○○○○と言われることが多く、
自分自身も相手の方を喜ばせたり楽しませたりすることが好きです。

趣味は○○で、特に◎◎が大好きです！
お互いが好きなことを一緒に楽しめたらいいですね＾＾

お互いを思いやり、楽しい時も辛い時も
一緒に乗り越えていけたらと思っています。

どうぞよろしくお願いいたします。

Good evening, nice to meet you!
I'm __ years old, from __, and currently living in __.
My job is related to __.

Up until now I've been so busy with my job that I haven't though much about things like romance or marriage, but, recently I started thinking that I want to seriously konkatsu,
so I registered, thinking it would be nice to meet someone I could share time with.

I'm often told _____ by the people around me,
and I myself think that I would really like to bring a partner joy and fun times.

My interests are __, and I especially like __!
I would like it if we could do things we each like together :)

I hope we can make it through everything together, fun times and the harsh times,
with consideration for each other.

I respectfully request that you be kind to me.

Through this example, we can understand that good profile text ought to be pithy and dense with important information: age, hometown, current location, job, personality, hobbies, hopes. Elizabeth Stokoe's work on the stigma of singleness in British speed dating (2010) found that speed daters had difficulty justifying their singleness in conversation, especially if they lacked substantial romantic experience. In order to avoid the implication that something was *wrong* with them—that they didn't desire or couldn't commit properly to a partner—romantically inexperienced speed daters used work or travel as respectable reasons for not having a significant romantic history. In much the same way, in the relatively more stigmatized world of Japanese online konkatsu and koikatsu, the Zexy Enmusubi website offers the ready-made excuse of a busy work life to explain both why its users might still be single, and why they've turned to the internet as a resource. It encourages people to say positive things about their personalities and what they think they can offer a partner, in terms of sharing common interests and the kind of emotional or pragmatic approaches they might have toward a long-term partnership. Then, it concludes with the common Japanese phrase *dōzo yoroshiku onegai itashimasu*, a hyperpolite formula that I have translated fairly literally above as "I respectfully request that you be kind to me." This formula tends to conclude both self-introductions and requests, and an online profile is both. It ends the profile in a way that asks the reader directly for a continuing and mutually beneficial acquaintance.

Indeed, in spite of the dramatic variation in profile structures, one thing seems to be constant, and that is politeness—up to a point. Many varieties of Japanese have a number of different linguistic resources for demonstrating respect to both interlocutors and to people being referenced: teineigo (polite language) and keigo (honorific language), respectively. In the example from Zexy Enmusubi above, all sentence-final verbs use polite forms, and where references are made to the profile viewers or their actions, the template also uses honorific forms. All of the sample profiles are as rigorously polite and, like this one, avoid first- and second-person pronouns entirely, which is frequently grammatically possible in Japanese. Avoiding pronouns also tends to sound more appropriately self-effacing, and avoids the sociolinguistic conundrum of having to choose *which* pronoun to use, with all of the baggage any particular pronoun entails.[22] Only one specifically mentions wanting a "wife" (*oku-san*); the rest use only gender-neutral terms like *kata*, the honorific word for "person," or *aite*, which simply means "partner," and, depending on the context, can mean anything from a date to a sports rival.

Being polite has consequences for how gender manifests in written (and spoken) Japanese. In 2017, with two research assistants, I carried out a large survey of profiles from Zexy Enmusubi—172 in total, 87 from men and 85 from women—and coded them for various linguistic and content features. When constructing profiles, nearly all users in our initial database wrote in a very standardly polite style, using polite language, but mostly avoiding the more elaborate honorifics often associated with women's speech. Equally absent are the more plain, "rough" forms said to characterize "men's speech." What the writers of these profiles imagine to be most appealing to the reader, then, is not heavily gender-dichotomized speech, but polite speech that works to minimize gender differences. This is unsurprising, given my earlier findings about ideologies of polite conversation among matchmakers.

As a result, when coding these profiles, we didn't code for first-person and second-person pronouns, or sentence-final particles, even though these are some of the most highly gendered linguistic forms. This is primarily because we didn't really need to. In a more in-depth qualitative analysis of thirty different men's profiles that I conducted separately, only four used first-person pronouns at all, and each of them only used a pronoun once throughout their "self-introduction." Three of these were the gently masculine "boku," but one person even used the more formal "watashi." These results are in line with the sample profile text presented directly above, written in a highly gender-neutral style that mostly avoids pronouns. Similarly, sentence-final particles, another strongly gendered form, were almost wholly absent, save for the occasional "ne" or "na" (which mark tag questions) or, for one user, "ka nā," which expresses a feeling of wondering about something. Neither of these forms is especially gendered—if anything, "ne" leans slightly feminine.

A similar analysis that I conducted of thirty women's profiles revealed an almost identical avoidance of pronominal forms—no second person pronouns, and only two women who used first person pronouns (the formal watashi). All the women were polite to about the same degree as the men—in some instances, they may have actually been more rude, as a few women's profiles had codas apologizing for the preemptory rudeness of refusing to entertain messages from some kinds of men (such as men more than ten years older than themselves). Given this lack of gendered difference in language, the "hetero" in "heterosexuality" is plainly not to be found in the linguistic form of Zexy Enmusubi profiles. However, given the interrelation of politeness and gender in Japanese, it shouldn't be surprising that most users choose to write in a fairly polite register when presenting themselves online to strangers, with the hope that anyone viewing their profile will evaluate them favorably. So, if it is not in the linguistic form, is there anywhere that we can find gender differences in these profiles?

Dalton and Dales (2016) found that "traditional" post-marriage gender roles in online konkatsu are reinforced by the "success stories" posted on the websites, where men and women who've successfully married share their happiness with the reader. They especially focus on the role of women as cooks for men, and the implications of this for the gendered division of labor in the household. And indeed, where gender differences make themselves felt in my qualitative analysis of Zexy Enmusubi profiles is in the different activities that men and women describe themselves as enjoying or frequently doing. These differences are subtle. They rarely impact what men and women say they want in a relationship, for example. Ideal relationships are based on mutual respect, talking openly to one another, joint activities, and overcoming challenges together—this is true for men and women alike. However, their given hobbies suggest gendered patterns of activity, in some ways that they may imagine continuing into their marriage. For example, eating delicious foods is a hobby frequently mentioned by both men and women—nearly half the men (13/30) include it as a hobby or favorite activity in some form or another, and some minority of these men actively cook (including one user who imagines a marriage where he cooks together with his partner). Food was popular among women too (16/30 users mentioned it), but fully one-third also specifically mentioned their cooking, and a couple also referenced skill at housework, which no man mentioned at all. Sports are another very frequently cited hobby, with many men and women engaging in the same popular sports—tennis, golf, mountain climbing, etc. However, small gender differences persist here too. While the women seem to generally be as active as the men, only women ever mention doing yoga. One final notable difference between men's and women's profiles on Zexy Enmusubi is that a few women (four) specifically mentioned they want to *amaeru*—a verb that expresses a desire to be dependent on someone, to be taken care of by them—to cuddle up to, and to be held, literally and metaphorically.

What all of this suggests is that gendered differences do manifest in users' self-presentations, in the form of subtle but meaningful differences in "appropriate" activities for men and women, and in the willingness of some women to express a desire to be emotionally vulnerable and reliant on her partner. However, all sixty profiles were also consistently polite, overwhelmingly refer to wanting to share or try out a partner's hobbies, and emphasize relationships based on mutual support and respect. In these profiles, a gender-minimal, companionate ideal of marriage seems to reign supreme, and the language of these profiles, rather than emphasizing gender difference or hierarchy, emphasize an approach to the other, a valuing and exploration of the other, that is reflected in gender-neutral, polite prose.

I have focused here heavily on Zexy Enmusubi, in part because it encourages clients so clearly to write—it's an ideal target for analyzing Japanese konkatsu users' linguistic content and style. However, a qualitative analysis of similar numbers of profiles on Tinder and the gay app Nine Monsters reveals that this style is fairly universal to user-generated linguistic context on partner matching platforms. Pronouns are avoided; verbs are polite. Most words for people are gender neutral. What tends to vary is not the style, but, especially on Tinder, whether users write at all. This also doesn't seem to be gendered, with similar numbers of male and female users leaving their profiles blank. When Tinder users do write anything, it tends to be shorter and bubblier—perhaps just a line or two, peppered with emoji. Longer profiles, however, follow the basic pattern of talking about hobbies and potential shared activities, whether it be a serious relationship, or the dubious offer of meeting for a casual drink together. Slowly, a distinct genre of profile writing *does* seem to be emerging, through the collective efforts of Japanese singles online, and the emerging norms and guidance provided by partner matching services.

CONCLUSION

It can be difficult to pinpoint what exactly might be the difference between "online" and "offline" modes of looking for a partner—between neotraditional matchmaking and more novel forms of konkatsu and koikatsu. Apps might offer or advertise in-person parties for meeting others, counseling services, or physical locations where users can get help, while, as noted earlier, matchmakers put profiles in online databases and communicate with their clients largely over text and email. The real difference seems to be in the amount of intermediary phatic labor involved. Matchmakers will speak on behalf of their clients, in addition to being present for initial introductions at the start of an omiai. Matchmakers also do less visible phatic labor in terms of filtering out potential connections by screening profiles for their clients and either suggesting or counseling against omiai with one client or another. Perhaps the real difference between the online and the offline, then, is in whether the mediating roles are played by humans or software, and whether the rules are enforced by humans or code. The differences in user experience are then not really a difference in the actual services offered, but in the different kinds of interaction and expectations fostered by different platforms. Online services generally have low barriers to entry, less, if any, human mediation, and a diversity of matching styles suiting a diverse community of users. This allows them to be appealingly self-directed and, far more so than any matchmaking service, *big*. For some, this casual and expansive set-up turns out to be a pleasurable advantage, while others discover that they actually prefer a more structured experience. Regardless of what users learn that they like, however, it seems that many Japanese singles are willing to give the internet a try. After all, there is very little to lose, a great deal to learn, and potentially much to gain.

NOTES

1. This page contains no original date of publication, but Archive.org has records of it from between 2005 and 2019, and it can still be viewed there: https://web.archive.org/web/20190409121830/http://www.pref.kyoto.jp/fukei/anzen/shonen_s/deai/index.html

2. According to official company information available at https://about.fb.com/company-info/ and https://sns.mixi.co.jp/service.html

3. https://www.bridge-lounge.jp/concept/

4. https://www.resally.jp/

5. The two readings of 恋 are the Japanese reading *koi*, as in *koibito*, "lover," and the Sino-Japanese *ren*, as in *ren'ai*, "romantic love." "Koikatsu" is unusual in that it combines a Japanese reading (*koi*), with a second character that has a Sino-Japanese reading (*katsu*). Usually compound words in Japanese are pronounced either with entirely Japanese readings or entirely Sino-Japanese readings. Therefore one might very reasonably expect the word to be pronounced "renkatsu." "Koikatsu," however, has a more obvious sonic play on "konkatsu." Many thanks to Keiko Nishimura for being pedantic and wonderful with me as we figured out this new word.

6. Research comparing these two cases is in progress, in collaboration with Makhabbat Boranbay.

7. The city was formally renamed to "Nur-Sultan" in 2019 following the resignation of Kazakhstan's first (and until then, only) president, Nursultan Nazarbayev. However, the name "Astana" (Kazakh for "capital") is still in common currency.

8. This claim is based on personal experience as a researcher using Tinder in a variety of contexts. Students in sociology and Eurasian studies at my home institution, Nazarbayev University, are producing some of the first work on online dating in Central Asia.

9. The site I've studied most extensively, Zexy Enmusubi, is only available in Japanese, as is YouBride. Omiai initially offered Japanese and English, but later removed the English option. jp.match.com only offers Japanese as well, despite being a localized version of an international platform. Pairs, another app mentioned frequently in my interviews, is also only available in Japanese. Domestically produced apps assume a linguistically homogeneous Japanese audience.

10. Many thanks to Makhabbat Boranbay for suggesting this interpretation in our discussions of Tinder in Japan and Kazakhstan.

11. Somewhat predictably, COVID-19 has affected my communication with research participants, in addition to the vast changes many of us have been making around the world to our broader social habits.

12. A bit over $20 US.

13. Tinder's support documents can be found at https://www.help.tinder.com/hc/ja, while the blog can be found at https://blog.gotinder.com/?locale=ja.

14. Information about Tinder's reporting tools and automated safety tools can be found at https://www.gotinder.com/safety-and-policy?locale=ja. The safety tips and tricks are at https://www.gotinder.com/safety?locale=ja.

15. https://youbride.jp/guide/

16. YouBride's safety information is located at https://youbride.jp/guide/safe. Zexy Enmusubi bundles safety information into the broader FAQ page: https://zexy-enmusubi.net/faq/.

17. According to results from the CiNii database and Google Scholar, scholarly articles on the topic of personal ads in Japan go back to the late 1990s at the earliest—a time already in the internet era. Many deal with internet sites facilitating the meetings of gay men. Moreover, the most closely corresponding term in Japanese, *kojin kōkoku* ("individual advertisement"), is a bit more like a "classified ad"

than a personal ad, so articles in Japanese on this topic are often about advertising more broadly. For example, most of the results for a search for "kojin kōkoku" on CiNii were from the legal journal *Liberty and Justice*, about the ethics of lawyers taking out personal advertisements.

18. My thanks to an anonymous reviewer for this suggestion.

19. https://www.help.tinder.com/hc/ja/articles/115003339043-プロフィールを編集する-

20. https://www.pairs.lv/pairs_manual/05/

21. This is not to imply that the genre of the online dating profile in English is static. It is probably impossible to calculate the influence that geolocation-based, photo-heavy services like Grindr and Tinder have had on more "traditional," text-oriented models of online dating profiles exemplified by older services like Match.com or OKCupid that more closely resembled newspaper personals. Changing legal frameworks also need to be considered. The sites that have most closely mimicked the newspaper personal ad, like Craigslist, became prominent targets of anti-human-trafficking campaigns and legislation in the US, and subsequently were forced to either shut down or remove the option to post personal ads seeking romantic or sexual partners (Thacker and boyd 2013).

22. This includes the gender implications of pronoun choices, the implied relationship implications of pronoun choices, and also the regional implications of pronoun choices. Hendry (1992) and Sunaoshi (2004) both discuss how the lack of "Standard Japanese" pronoun systems and honorific verb systems in some regional varieties of Japanese impact (especially female) speakers' abilities to be polite and to gender themselves appropriately.

5

✝

Structural Problems, Phatic "Solutions"

Having addressed the details of how Japanese singles, matchmakers, and companies have developed various kinds of phatic systems to encourage partnering and family formation, we now return to the broader issue of phatic communication. As singles construct their online self-representations, they are tasked with figuring out what kind of language stands the best chance of creating contact, of reaching out and touching the reader through the screen. The answer seems to be one that prioritizes politeness, and one that is conatively focused on appealing to the addressee through the specific use of addressee-honorific (teineigo) forms, the result of which tends to be a gender-neutral linguistic style. Domestically produced online platforms in Japan, as well as matchmaking agencies, provide their clients with a great deal of assistance in assembling an appropriately polite and appealing profile in the form of in-person counseling, help documentation, photographic advice, and referrals to professionals, among other things.[1] Those who opt to use international platforms are left more on their own, as these platforms are often designed with the idea that users already know what a profile should look like, or what kind of photo to upload. Even international apps that *do* offer more comprehensive user information might not offer it in Japanese. Scrolling down Bumble's front page in Japanese provides basic information about the app, but then quickly transitions to magazine-type articles in English about the effects of Mercury retrograde on relationships. Their array of advice and musings on a wide variety of app- and dating-related topics doubtless helps English-speaking users, but the same wealth of knowledge isn't available to all users worldwide.

Meanwhile, Japanese society, in continually constructing and reconstructing itself, has to figure out just how much phaticity can do. It is not an accident that most of matchmakers' labor centers around giving advice about how to interact with prospective marriage partners. It is also not an accident that domestically-produced Japanese partner matching services are more invested in teaching their users how to interact in much more substantial ways than internationally-developed sites are. Even when international platforms have well-developed Japanese-language interfaces and documentation, they may still not have culturally relevant knowledge about the history—or lack thereof—of personal ads and online dating in Japan, which is to say, they may not know what their users don't know about how to effectively use a partner matching platform. Yamada and Shirakawa (2008), in their original statement of the necessity of konkatsu, largely blamed shifting cultural factors for lower marriage rates and later ages at first marriage, such as the collapse of omiai and workplace introductions, the pressures on women to marry men of a higher social status than themselves, and a "relaxed" system of romance that privileges individual choice and that does not assume that dating automatically leads to marriage. But a lack of phatic *savoir faire* or the will to make a commitment aren't the only or perhaps even the primary reasons for marrying later in life, or maybe never marrying at all. There are also plainly a number of structural factors standing between Japanese singles and family formation that mostly amount to too much work, for too little pay, and with not enough help—especially for women, whether or not they have children.

Because of the broader political and economic implications of Japan's advanced demographic crisis, the government has taken a number of concrete steps to improve work/life balance possibilities for working mothers. However, given the low rates of illegitimacy in Japan, such working mothers are overwhelmingly married (or divorced). The never-married have children only very rarely.[2] It is surprising, then, that the Japanese government has done far less to encourage singles to marry. While the structural dimensions of married couples' problems have been met with legal reforms and childcare infrastructure—even if these things are perhaps not always culturally appropriate, or not usefully applied—the scale and nature of the problem and the proposed solutions basically match. But the structural barriers between singles and marriage have not been met with similar, appropriate structural solutions. Rather, singles face emotional pleas and calls for individual action. The prescription for Japan's ills is for individuals to "marriage hunt," not for society more broadly to secure rights for workers or a living wage.

However, one factor that might make phatic labor seem like a reasonable solution to Japan's marriage and birth rate problems is that, as discourses about shifting ideals of masculinity in Japan illustrate, changes in Japan's social structure over the last twenty or thirty years have been credited with concomitant changes, not only in the opportunities available to young men but also in their very personalities. Lack of opportunity for stable employment and advancement in their careers is supposed to incline them to be more generally domestic, less ambitious at work, and disinterested in (straight) sex or (heterosexual romantic) relationships (Ushikubo 2008).[3] According to the arguments made about herbivorous men, "the kids these days" are not only more out of touch, but less able to remedy their situation, or even disposed to see it as a problem. If this is true, then it behooves social commentators like Yamada Masahiro to sound the alarm and alert the youth of the need to take action.

In this chapter, I argue that phatic techniques and technologies like online partner matching or more traditional matchmaking services can probably play some useful role in helping Japanese singles find partners. However, it also seems plain that there are limits to how much change individual action is capable of effecting on a society-wide scale. Based on the data already presented, we can safely say that offline konkatsu practices have become normalized. Meanwhile, the online outcroppings of the marriage (and dating) industry are undergoing similar normalization processes, in part due to changing norms of internet use, and in part through changing terminologies that shift "love activities" into the realm of the respectable. While at present many singles may be shy about admitting they use these services, using them also seemed to be obvious to my interviewees, the thing to do for people who want to find romantic relationships. While the language of matchmaking and online platforms may be fairly androgynous, it stops at language. Matchmaking does build a "separate spheres" vision of masculinity, femininity, and spousal relations into its system. It presumes the obviousness of heterosexuality, the naturalness of it, and the likewise apparent obviousness of male breadwinner/female homemaker model of gendered labor division, even while it also encourages mutual understanding, perspective-taking, and explicit negotiation of emotions and relationships between men and women. The diversity of online partner matching apps, by contrast, might be able to empower people who have different visions of marriage and relationships. However, the development of easy, entertaining, and inexpensive tools for meeting people, or for imagining different relationship forms, is probably not enough to encourage substantially more relationship formation, marriage, and childbearing in the face of the very valid material conditions that lead many single Japanese to avoid relationships.

THE ALLURE OF THE PHATIC

Why do phatic solutions to structural problems seem so compelling? In part, I suspect it is simply because they do not threaten established interests. Leonard Schoppa (2020), in a recent summary of Japanese policy attempts to fix declining fertility rates over the last thirty years, accuses governmental actors of "relying on logic and hope over evidence," as per the title of his paper. For Schoppa, the evidence suggests that Japan's fertility rates will not rise without a serious overhaul of the demands that Japanese employers make on their workers, and a serious liberalization in thinking about family, including more expansive notions of gender roles and a full embrace of alternative, nonmarital family forms. But instead of rethinking the Japanese labor system as a whole structure, Japanese policy has largely focused on supplements to the existing employment system, like expanding childcare options. This is very human: large-scale social engineering projects are rightfully a bit terrifying. Revolutions are unpleasant and uncertain things, even for the people who want them.

However, I think there is also a deeper reason, which is to do with understandings of heterosexual desire and how it underpins institutions like marriage in Japan. Machado (2020) writes that, despite the silence of legal scholars on the issue of same-sex marriage in recent years, late nineteenth-century legal scholars writing and interpreting Japan's new, Western-influenced Meiji Civil Code explicitly addressed the issue of same-sex marriage and put forth legal principles to explain why it could not possibly be legal under these laws. Legal scholar Frank Upham notes that same-sex marriage is legal in "virtually all affluent democracies" save Japan (2021, 196). He also notes that this is somewhat mysterious, because Japan has an extensively documented history of not only tolerating, but *valorizing* sexual relations between men prior to Westernization, and, moreover, has never been predominantly a Christian or Muslim country. Consequently, the religious objections against same-sex marriage that carry such weight elsewhere, based on passages in the Hebrew Bible, Christian writings, and the Quran, are of little concern for most Japanese.

The argument against same-sex marriage seems to not be about morality, then, but rather about the foundations of the Japanese social order in kin relations. S. P. F. Dale points to the family registry system in Japan (*koseki*), which records births, deaths, and marriages, and functions as a primary form of identification the way a birth certificate might elsewhere. But critically, unlike a birth certificate, the koseki documents a *family*, not an individual. Consequently, "Japanese citizens are citizens in the context of being a member of a family unit" (2020, 145). The heterosexual, reproductive family is inseparable from individual identity and political belonging. Dale also argues that the koseki system "encourages a form of institutional performativity—of making one's relationship fit the legal configurations of what is allowed—regardless of the nature of the relationship itself" (148). Consequently, same-sex partners might secure rights for their relationship via an adult adoption, despite their romantic relationship or domestic partnership bearing no resemblance to a parent/child relationship.[4] The objection to same-sex marriage in Japan thus seems to be rooted in beliefs about "normalcy" and "reproductivity." A same-sex marriage is just utterly illegible to the system.

Both the issue of same-sex marriage and the problem of increasing rates of late marriage and non-marriage reveal another common assumption about heterosexuality, which is that it is something that, in ordinary circumstances, "just happens" when men and women are in proximity to each other. In Megumi Ushikubo's description of herbivore men, one passage that stands out rather dramatically right at the beginning is when she describes the strangeness of young men who can platonically share hotel rooms with young women, *and somehow not have sex with them*. The idea that a man and a woman, alone together in a room, could simply sleep, rest, or have non-sexual fun, seems incomprehensible to her (2008, 5), and dramatizes the deviance of the herbivores. But this folk understanding of heterosexuality and heterosexual desire is deeply lacking. Heterosexual desire does not simply appear between any man and any woman left in proximity for sufficient time, compelling them to act. Julienne Obadia, writing precisely about proximity, notes that proximity is associated with highly valued forms of intimacy—"true love" and "chosen family." However, we cannot assume that proximity leads directly to intimacy. Rather, she argues that "attention to proximity . . . allows us to identify the affective entanglements of assembled, clustered persons while foregrounding the possibility that proximity might generate distance, misrecognition, or isolation more powerfully than anything else" (2020, 1330–1331). In other words, while people tend to have emotional reactions to being near each other, it's just as possible that the presence of another person might make us feel even more alone, rather than straightforwardly encouraging connection and warm feelings. Obadia also points to Malinowski's view of ethnography as the generation of knowledge based on simply being near to one's research subjects, every day, in the same way that Malinowski also argued that "phatic communion" followed from interaction. We can therefore understand "proximity" in much the same way we can understand "phaticity." Just as communicative connection does not always engender positive social interactions or relationships, mere physical nearness does not always beget connection.

Moreover, feminist scholars pointed out rather long ago that "heterosexuality" is really too broad a term that doesn't adequately specify anyone's sexual orientation in a meaningful way. Desire is always more narrow, more specific than just "anyone of the opposite sex." Nancy Chodorow, in discussing the narrowness of sexual desire, suggests replacing terms like "heterosexual" with "tall-blond-Wasposexual," "short-curly-haired zaftig Jewishosexual," and "African-American-with-a-southern-accent-sexual," concluding that ultimately "biology cannot explain the content of either cultural fantasy or private eroticism" (Chodorow 1994, 38). Our individual histories, our personal dispositions, our individual locations in particular cultural formations, and our participation in broader cultural discourses all influence the specific kinds of partners that any particular person might desire, as well as their actual behavior in pursuing or avoiding some kinds of partners.

Larger social institutions, such as kinship structures, may also play a role in regimenting which persons are available as appropriate objects of (heterosexual) desire. Gayle Rubin notes that

> Kinship systems do not merely encourage heterosexuality to the detriment of homosexuality. In the first place, specific forms of heterosexuality may be required. For instance, some marriage systems have a rule of obligatory cross-cousin marriage. A person in such a system is not only heterosexual but "cross-cousin-sexual." If the rule of marriage further specifies matrilateral cross-cousin marriage, then a man will be "mother's-brother's-daughter-sexual" and a woman will be "father's-sister's-son-sexual" (Rubin 1975, 180–181).

In Rubin's analysis, both incest taboos as well as preferred or obligatory marriage patterns in a society direct or deflect desire in particular directions, toward or away from people who are in specific relationships to us. Japan provides theorists of gender and sexuality with an interesting case study of the in/evitability of heterosexual pairing, given its long years of low birth rates and steady increase in the percentage of the population who never marry (Retherford et al. 2001). One-person households are now the norm in Japan, a trend that parallels that of many other developed nations (Raymo 2015). Heterosexual relationships are simply not "just happening." Phatic solutions may seem like they will work largely because of an underlying belief that simply putting men and women into contact with each other will lead to the formation of romantic attachments, will turn one-person households into two-person families. But this misunderstands both the effects of proximity and the specificity of individual sexual desire.

The data on marriage rates in Japan and in other developed countries supports this analysis. Since I began my earliest fieldwork in 2007, rates of singleness have only increased. In 2005, 52.2 percent of never-married men and 44.7 percent of never-married women had no opposite-sex romantic relationships, while by 2015, these percentages had risen to 69.8

percent and 59.1 percent, respectively (NIPSSR 2017, 12). Tomomi Yama-guchi, an anthropologist of gender and sexuality in Japan, has pointed out that the government survey that this data comes from is deeply flawed, insofar as it ignores the experiences of divorced people, widows, unwed parents, and LGBTQ+ people. The data is flawed because the survey it is based on comes from a very particular vision of not just heterosexual-ity but heteronormativity in Japan. It is also flawed because it exists as a guide for the state to diagnose the romantic and sexual malaise of a popu-lace that needs to have more sex, and within the confines of heterosexual marriage relations, to have more (legitimate, Japanese) children (2016).

That said, the decline in sex and relationships does also seem to be *real* among the populations that most concern the Japanese government, and declines in sexual activity have been observed worldwide. In other writ-ing, Yamaguchi has pointed out that the desire to characterize sexlessness in Japan as an "exotic" phenomenon is both unfair and Orientalist, given that the same trends that we can see in Japan are also visible in Britain (McCurry 2016). In the case of Britain, reduced levels of sexual activity are portrayed as a matter of understandable factors like overwork; in the case of Japan, the same thing is held up as evidence of the mysterious, topsy-turvy nature of Japanese society and culture. What Yamaguchi sug-gests—and I agree—is that actually, the same factors are likely at work in both places. I would add that when we look at Britain or the United States, we see this decline in sexual activity happening in environments that already have a robust phatic infrastructure and social acceptance of online dating. This suggests that phatic labor and phatic technologies probably play a limited role in encouraging either sex *per se* or pairing on a larger scale. For example, in the United States, online dating has been the single most popular way to meet a partner since 2013, and has been displacing introductions via friends since the 1990s (Rosenfeld et al. 2019). However, the frequency of sex in the United States declined dur-ing the same period, while the number of people not in relationships rose (Twenge et al. 2017). Thus, while building phatic infrastructures may be helpful in some respects, changing the romantic and sexual landscape of a country also requires effective policy changes that support both singles and families in concrete economic ways, or that look to solve population problems non-biologically, for example, through increased immigration.

THE LIMITS OF THE PHATIC

In addition to heteronormative assumptions about contact between men and women, another reason why phatic solutions seem eminently reason-able is that so many people in Japan state the problem of finding a partner in phatic terms. A refrain constantly cited in discourses about matchmaking and konkatsu—a refrain with no particular source—is *(ii) deai ga nai*: "there aren't any (good) encounters" or more colloquially, "I'm just not meeting anyone (nice)." Yamada and Shirakawa (2008), in their invention of konkatsu, tie this to changes in Japan's economic systems that have not yet resulted in changes in men's and women's consciousness, in their sense of who is desirable, or marriageable, or what a marriage looks like. They argue that women still desire men who can provide for them, but point out that men with sufficient incomes to singlehandedly support a family, who are also under forty, are tremendously rare. They note that men still lack basic homemaking skills, but also need wives to work, because a single income is insufficient for a comfortable family life. This puts women in the position of doing everything at home while *also* working—what is classically referred to as the "second shift" that women work after getting home from paid outside employment (Hochschild and Machung 2003). As a result, most people appear inadequate as potential partners to most other people. No one is able to give enough at work or at home to enable some more manageable division of labor, whether that be sharing the housework and wage work equally, or enabling one partner to stay home full-time.

Of course, Yamada and Shirakawa also link this to the fact that individual choice of partners has become normative. In the past (prior to the 1980s), marriage partners would have been chosen by parents or limited by the number of suitable available singles in one's social circles. The demise of these systems leaves mating choices up to perpetually dissatisfied individuals whose models of how things *should be* are painfully inadequate to cope with how they *are*. They explicitly draw a parallel to employment: in "premodern society" (*zenkindai shakai*), men would have inherited their fathers' occupations, and women would have been married to men with jobs much like those of their fathers. But just as greater choice of jobs has resulted in job shortages, personal dissatisfaction, and endless job hunting, so too has greater choice of spouses resulted in later marriage across the board and an increasing number of people who never marry at all, even when they *want* to (2008, 12–18).

Other research, covered earlier, largely backs up Yamada and Shirakawa's claims. Men don't make enough to support families as sole breadwinners, but generally don't support their wives in housework or childcare either. Women feel pressured to stop working when they have children, but know that there's a lack of financial and social support to help them stay home, and aren't always prepared to reconcile themselves to the sacrifices demanded of them by husbands, children, and broader social expectations of wives and mothers. Women also typically expect to "marry up," or at least marry equal, in terms of their partners' incomes or educational achievement, such that most women, regardless of their own backgrounds or ability to support themselves, desire partners from a very limited social class of men. And so we return to the question: Who exactly is supposed to want to marry whom?

Yamada and Shirakawa recommend conscious, intentional, individual searching for a marriage partner, without expecting a partner to just appear or marriage to just sort of happen, as a solution to the problems they outline. In a "comic book essay" aimed at a female audience that was published shortly after *The Age of "Marriage Hunting,"* Shirakawa advises marriage hunters to talk to a variety of married people they know about their lifestyles, in order to realize that married life doesn't take a single form, but rather, consists of a process of negotiating life together as a couple (Shirakawa and Tada 2008, 47–56). I take her point to be that successful konkatsu is not based on any particular activity so much as it is, again, based on a shift in consciousness—an awareness of the need for conscious effort to find a partner, coupled with an awareness of diversity in marriage forms beyond the male breadwinner model. Partner matching services might promise meaningful introductions to good people, but one of the points of konkatsu, a point that has been missed in much of the broader discourse around it, is that anyone engaging in konkatsu needs to rethink what "good" means. That is to say, what sounds like a *phatic* problem—a problem of connection, or its absence—is actually a problem of *perception*, of the clash of ideals and reality, of norms forged in a Fordist economic system that can no longer be relied on, all of which must be sorted out prior to any phatic stage of marriage hunting.

I have found that matchmakers are primarily pragmatists. They are keenly aware that most of their clients are looking for someone impossible, and as a result, much of their counseling in the pre-omiai stage involves getting clients to focus on who they can realistically expect to meet. Hence, we have Yamada Yumiko's brutal calculations, cited in chapter 3, of how much male income can be traded for how much female youth. On the one hand, the lesson that this post teaches its readers is that youth and income can be exchanged for each other. A more subtle lesson, and the one I think she was *actually* trying to impart, is that most men and women need to be more realistic about who they can attract. The NNK has recognized the decreasing number of men with stable, breadwinner-level incomes over the last few years by allowing men with precarious employment to sign up; previously, only men who were regular, full-time employees (*seishain*), or professionals like doctors and lawyers, were eligible to join. Ergo, most men might want to think twice before messaging the youngest hotties in the database. They need to think realistically about who will be interested in what they have to offer. Most women will likewise not be fabulously young and pretty, which also amounts to them having less to "trade" in order to land the most wealthy (but still reasonably young) men they find in their searches. Consequently, everyone needs to lower their expectations of the men or women they might meet.

The theme of lowered or limited expectations resonates through countless interviews and meetings and training sessions with matchmakers: so much of client counseling amounts to reorienting their expectations and training them to focus clearly on a very few absolutely necessary criteria for a partner, rather than looking for someone perfect, or fixating on criteria that are incredibly difficult for most clients to meet. In the words of Sugawara-sensei:

> Everyone comes in with, holding onto, these high ideals. Like really, a prince is going to appear. But, humans, of course I think this applies to me, this applies to everybody but, there's no such thing as a person who's one-hundred percent perfect. I'm the same way, there's absolutely no man out there who's one hundred percent my ideal person, so, how much are you willing to forgive (*yuruseru*)? You might say. The ones who know how much they can forgive in a partner, who understand that, and really make an effort, for their partners, to understand the other person: they'll successfully marry.

Partner matching strategies clearly vary in the extent to which they are able to inculcate this consciousness shift, and as we can infer from looking at the low success rates for matchmaking, even practices that deliberately try to shift client consciousness don't actually result in marriage for most people. To the extent that partner matching services are phatic technologies and practices of phatic labor, they can be used to reach out to people. But they cannot necessarily ensure that their clients or their users are making practical choices about whom to contact. Moreover, to the extent that partner matching services reify the male-breadwinner model in the data structures or technological affordances built into them, they may actually be counterproductive in some ways. Matchmakers might encourage their clients to be practical and open-minded, but listing income only on men's profiles structurally embeds the importance of a man's income into the database itself, while literally erasing women's potential monetary contributions to the household.

Individual selfishness, reclusiveness, lack of ambition, lack of effort, and generational sexual malaise have all been cited as reasons why Japanese singles are reluctant to marry, but by looking at this question of what counts as meeting someone "good," we can see how structural considerations become personal, how they make marriage and childbearing *feel* impossible, and, factually speaking, *do* make them incredibly difficult, because so few people seem "good" to each other. And so few people *seem* "good" because so few people *are* good, by either the standards of the middle of the twentieth century, or the shifting standards of the present. New families need financial and practical support, and often enough, they do not have either. Consequently, a change in consciousness, a reevaluation of what a marriage could look like, in addition to phatic labor—the konkatsu formula—is unlikely to present as a meaningful response to the problems of intimacy, family, and reproduction that it is meant to solve. Moreover, as flawed as the results of Japanese governmental surveys might be, they also indicate that the practices of married couples *have* changed, moving away from the male breadwinner model if only due to straightforward economic necessity. Most single women surveyed (66.9%) expect to work after marriage, and even more single men expect their future wives to work in some capacity (71.3%) (NIPSSR 2017, 17–18). These expectations are borne out by practice: 73 percent of women do continue working after marriage, which is to say, the majority of married couples live in two-income households (34). The consciousness shift *has happened already*, and seems to be solidifying itself as relatively affordable konkatsu and koikatsu services make themselves ever more available.

I do not wish to suggest that the partner matching industry, in its various guises, has no useful role to play. If nothing else, the ability to meet and set up matches online via the ever-present phone in one's pocket has the potential to help mitigate issues of busyness and fatigue. As an anthropologist, I am loath to suggest that humans are rational economic actors, but in this case, they really do seem to be. The world of konkatsu and omiai exists to encourage reluctant singles to participate in heteronormative transitions to adulthood, without acknowledging that the current state of Japanese society has effectively disincentivized heterosexual engagement, or at least, disincentivized the kinds of heteronormative, marriage-oriented relationships that Japanese sociology and policy hopes to promote.

MATERIAL CONSTRAINTS

Over and over, the structure of labor intrudes into phatic possibilities in various ways. Misato found that a partner appeared for her almost magically around the same time that her job eased up on her, giving her more time—one of the basic constraints on singles who would prefer not to be. People who don't have time, don't have time. Japan is famous for its demanding labor culture, with long hours and little in the way of vacation—although as of 2018, at 1,680 hours per worker per year, it's actually below the OECD (2020) average of 1,734 hours and the US average of 1,786 hours. Nonetheless, "death from overwork" (*karōshi*) is a repeated topic of popular discourse, news, and legislation (Kanai 2008). Moreover,

while Japan's overall average working hours may not be so high according to the OECD, "the proportion of individuals working excessive hours
(>45 hours per week) has become significantly higher in Asia than in
Western countries" (Eguchi et al. 2016, e313). Moreover, the incentives
provided by "meritocratic" workplace reforms now lead to employees
performing unpaid, unrecorded overtime by taking their work home with
them, so as to get everything done while also appearing efficient to their
employers (Gagné 2020, 75). In an environment where overwork literally
kills people, how are single Japanese realistically supposed to tend to
anything beyond mere survival?

The same unforgiving work environments that prevent Japanese singles from finding the time or energy to have romantic relationships are
also obstacles to marriage and family formation in other ways. Stagnating
wages and increased job precarity leave many singles feeling like they
don't have the means to support a family properly. Men, in particular,
may also feel unattractive to women because of their labor circumstances.
According to the 2015 Japanese National Fertility Survey (the most recent
comprehensive data available, with all its deficiencies, as pointed out
above), over 40 percent of both male and female single respondents selected "money for marriage" as the most substantial obstacle to their own
marital hopes (NIPSSR 2017, 9). Moreover, money, labor, and gender are
intimately related. Different kinds of work are imagined to be appropriate
for women and men, and different meanings are assigned to them. As we
have seen through matchmaking practices, only a man's ability to provide
"matters" in terms of family ideology, even if most households require
women's wage labor as well—even when the need for their labor is more
and more openly acknowledged.

If singles don't feel that they have enough money to get married, it
should not be difficult to imagine that this same lack of resources affects
decisions about whether to have children at all, and if so, how many. Lee
and Lee (2014) find that working *per se* doesn't impact women's decisions
to have (more) children, but childcare availability does. Despite governmental expansions of childcare systems, Japan still suffers from a short-
age of it, with many children on waitlists for places in care centers. Lee
and Lee focus specifically on childcare centers because other ostensible
childcare options, like nurseries and kindergartens, assume that mothers
are primarily at home and thus have inflexible and limited hours during
which they offer childcare and education, leaving parents (mothers) to
fill in the rest. So, despite the raw number of facilities that will look after
children for at least some of the day, few are actually useful for working
parents.

Japanese firms are also not particularly forgiving about maternity
leave, although the right to take such leave is legally protected. Brinton

and Mun (2016) examined the role played by HR managers in granting leave. While the managers that they interviewed approved of parental leave in *theory*, when employees actually made use of it, the HR managers perceived these employees as insufficiently committed to their jobs. They also expected workers who returned from parental leave to be as productive as before, and to work long hours, as before, as if nothing in their lives had changed, rather than anticipating that new parents might need more flexible schedules going forward to accommodate ongoing childcare. As a result, female employees who take parental leave (which male employees almost never do, despite being eligible) wind up in a situation where they are expected to be primary caretakers for their children *and* work long hours, and are incapable of doing both. Brinton and Mun conclude by wondering if parental leave actually functions in Japan as a way to reinforce the secondary nature of women's employment, rather than as a policy that serves to foster greater equality and possibilities in the workplace for women.

Where childcare facilities and workplaces fail, kin-based care can help families, but a combination of social stigma and practical difficulties conspire against women working while their children are young. Women's participation in employment in Japan has long been observed to have an "M-shaped" curve, when plotted against age, although the curve has softened in recent years. In early/mid-life, many women (33.9%) drop out of the labor market entirely to raise their children (NIPSSR 2017, 35). Nosaka (2009) finds that fertility is higher among working women whose own mothers who live nearby or are younger and more able to help with childcare; in-laws, that is, paternal grandparents, also frequently provide meaningful assistance that allows mothers to keep working. In the absence of childcare by one's own parents or in-laws, women often need to quit working, as no other childcare may be available. They are left to simply suffer through the resulting financial burdens.

My friend Akiko's pregnancy dramatized some of these issues as I was finishing up my dissertation in 2013. Before her pregnancy, her income, combined with her husband's, enabled them to live a comfortable middle-class life. Soon after she got pregnant, however, she started to feel that she had to quit her job in retail management, even though her husband's salary was really only enough for one person to live comfortably, let alone three. They had to move, leaving their apartment in upscale north-central Kyoto, and looked into public housing and other assistance programs. I saw her much less after that, in part because she lived so much farther away, on the rural north edge of town. While her husband's parents lived nearish to Kyoto and could provide some childcare assistance, her own parents lived several prefectures away, and were therefore of limited help. Several years later, she would tell me how uncomfortable she had initially felt with motherhood, how much it seemed to take from her life, and how much she really *resented* it for a long time. By contrast, our mutual friend Marie, who had her son a few months later, was only able to keep working because her own job had much more flexible hours, and because her parents also lived nearby. Unlike Akiko, she had reliable childcare and, after she divorced her husband, fallback housing.

WHAT PHATIC TECHNOLOGIES CAN ACTUALLY DO

In summary: the insurmountable-feeling problems facing Japanese singles are low pay; long hours at work; lack of support and help outside of family (who might not be available); and inflexible notions of family that require disproportionate sacrifices from women, and penalize alternative family structures. It should be obvious that no amount of matchmakers, however well-intentioned, can raise wages in Japan, make temporary contracts permanent, or create more social welcome for unmarried single mothers overnight. However, structural problems not only require structural solutions: they require structural solutions of the right scale and scope, aimed at the right problems. Some structural solutions aimed at helping working mothers have already been attempted, but without the results anticipated. Schoppa (2020) points out that the Japanese government *has* made substantial policy changes to strengthen parental leave policies, to extend the hours of childcare services, and to enable workers to have more flexible schedules, in order to reduce the opportunity costs of marriage and childbearing for women. They did so following OECD recommendations and international best practices, and on a timetable not too dissimilar from some European countries. But even in the face of these changes, birth rates are still declining.

We then have to ask, what makes Japan different to Europe? In spite of Brinton and Mun's findings regarding the profoundly imperfect implementation of childcare leave policies, it is not as if these policy changes have not helped at all. There were certainly more working mothers in Japan in the 2010s than in the 1990s, and Schoppa also notes that as of 2018, Japan had a higher percentage of women in the workforce than the United States or France. He goes on to suggest that the difference lies in norms of labor and family formation, with reference to the work of Miho Iwasawa: "The difference in overall fertility rates in France, Sweden, and the United States was entirely accounted for by the extra births taking place outside of marriage. If Japan really wanted to boost fertility rates . . . it needed to shift social norms (and perhaps some public policies) to become more welcoming and supportive of non-traditional families" (2020, 322). Women make decisions about fertility in the context of a world that continues to expect them to prioritize motherhood, perhaps all the more frantically so as birth rates sink and sink. But so long as the constraints of motherhood are sufficiently, well, constraining, Schoppa expects women to continue to opt out of the whole business, and quite reasonably so. Adding a courtyard to a house that really needs an extra bedroom will not solve the problem of how many people can live there. While structural solutions are necessary, they also have to make the *right* adjustments to social, political, and economic institutions.

It is in this respect that some phatic technologies may be able to make a difference. The government may be able to regulate how employers treat their employees, but it cannot singlehandedly change how people think about appropriate family structures and gender roles. One thing that delighted me when I first started looking at the structure of profiles on Zexy Enmusubi was the fact that, when giving clients options for choosing what they imagined their married life to look like, both men and women were able to say who (if anyone) they wanted to be the primary earner, who they wanted to take primary responsibility for chores and child-rearing, and both were given the option to declare that they envisioned having or being a *house-husband*, among other options. I confess that these are small details, but after years of researching matchmaking and konkatsu, I also found them completely astounding. I had never seen anything like it. The architects of Zexy Enmusubi had, first, considered that men might want to be professional homemakers, or that women might want husbands who stayed home, and then, second, *they built that consideration into their system*. A test search for men choosing this option turned up only a few hundred profiles, but it also turned up a few hundred profiles. Some men who are given this option are declaring it openly as part of their search for a partner. Even men who don't tick the house-husband box may benefit simply from seeing it listed as an option. In the context of Schoppa's analysis, it seems to me that there is value in simply *asking*, in not taking for granted which partner will bear which household responsibilities based on gender alone—even if some of the men who ticked the house-husband box seemed to have done so out of confusion, when I looked at their full profiles.

Linguistic anthropologists start from the assumption that language is multifunctional, and moreover, that many of these functions happen simultaneously, encoded in different aspects of the form of an utterance: the sound, the syntax, the pace of speech. We have also begun to consider that phatic language comes in what we might want to call different colors or different qualities. "Hello" may have almost no semantic meaning, may be purely phatic, but a sullen, half-audible hello is a different kind of contact than a hello that rings with loud excitement. "Hello" can be an angry shout at someone who isn't paying attention, or a terrified question launched into a dark and frightening space. Not only should we consider that there are both phatic violence and phatic communion, that there are phatic labor and obligations and fantasies, but that there are potentially innumerable qualities of contact enabled by phatic language.

Moreover, when we speak of these different qualities of phaticity, we are also speaking of the kind of relationship they presuppose. If contact is a precondition for interaction and relationship of some kind, then the kind of contact "sets the tone" for the interaction to follow. When Zuckerman (2016) discusses phatic violence, he is discussing relationships between competitors based on antagonism and hierarchy, winning and losing. When Nozawa (2015) speaks of the pleasures of being "without connection" (*muen*), he is talking about relief from the burdensome, obligatory kind of phatic work engendered by kin relations, work relations, neighborhood relations—the people you *must* stop and greet, interact with, and maintain relationships with in order to continue coexisting as part of the same family, workplace, or shared living area. So, too, do the phatic endeavors of Japanese singles have particular kinds of relationships presupposed by the way they are conducted—in this case, based on how different phatic technologies shape self-representation, how people can reach out to each other, proclaim their presence, and hope for a response.

As a matter of pure logic, presuppositions have entailments. Perhaps it is a wildly optimistic suggestion, but changing the way we can or must present ourselves to others might be able to encourage different kinds of relating by presuming a different structure of interaction that follows from contact. We can see clear examples of this happening in the history of social media. Facebook's policies that require users to use their legal names in profiles seem to have played a substantial role in reframing social media in Japan not so much as a separate "cyberspace," but as an extension of the real world, a logic that makes it as safe to put one's picture online as it is to go out in public. The interaction this entails is different than tweeting under a pseudonym on Twitter. Facebook is the online place where users collect all their offline people: classmates, friends, and coworkers past and present; extended family and in-laws. This same logic turns people we meet online into potential real-world friends, lovers, or spouses: how many flirtations begin on, or are enabled by, social media? So perhaps it is not too far-fetched to suggest that different kinds of profiles or messaging systems could have an effect on interactions between men and women that would otherwise be shaped by extant heteronormative practices that have all too ironically played a substantial role in discouraging heterosexual relationships. As the example of Zexy Enmusubi suggests, some websites may already be trying to do this. Bumble, by insisting that women in heterosexual matches must message men first, is doing it explicitly and consciously, with precisely the hope that better relationships will rise out of shifting the "usual" social role of conversation-initiator in a heterosexual pairing from the male party to the female party. Starting a conversation from a place of female desire and agency could entail interactions that might build on this, giving women more power in relationships from the start.

Research on other kinds of online interaction also teaches us that the structures we build, based on the people we assume are likely to use the software we design, can encourage or discourage particular kinds of communities. Games research, in particular, has been able to show how different kinds of communities arise out of different technological structures. For example, Pearce and Artemisia's study of players who formed communities based on the *Myst Online* game called *Uru* found equal numbers of men and women playing the game and participating in communities around it on message boards and in virtual worlds, which is incredibly rare for gaming communities. Most players were also middle-aged, and many players didn't otherwise game at all. Pearce argues that "to a certain extent, the game's own values and ideologies predispose it to attract a certain type of player, even before the game is actually played. Once those players come together, their community forms and develops around these shared values, which also intersect with the values embedded in the game itself" (2009, 73). *Myst* and *Uru* valued puzzle-solving, and *Uru* offered players realistic avatars that could even be customized to look old—a sharp contrast to most games. As a result, many players who perhaps felt alienated by more sensational, action-oriented, sexy, or violent games felt comfortable in the artistic, slow-paced, story-oriented worlds of *Myst* and *Uru*. This is then clearly reflected in the unusual (for gaming) demographics of the *Uru* player and fan community.

There is ample reason to believe that social networks might function similarly. The design of any platform—its profile creation options, its search options, its contact options—will, like the design of a game, build in certain values. Tinder's enormous pictures and sidelined text foreground appearances. Its mechanism of swiping right or left on the phone screen to express interest in someone or to dismiss them encourages rapid judgments of people based on quick visual semiotic assessments. Given this, it's not surprising that many Tinder users don't fill out their profile beyond uploading images, or that it has a widespread reputation as a hookup app, or as deai-kei. The structure of the app predisposes users to particular kinds of relatively superficial and rapid interaction and therefore, probably attracts and keeps users who are comfortable with that kind of interaction. The community and the local culture that grow up around the app are not *predetermined* by it, but are certainly *conditioned* by it. However, the cultures we build in particular digital spaces don't necessarily stay neatly contained there. Social networks that become popular have the ability to reshape how it is that we interact, or conceive of community. Daniel Miller argues that Facebook, as used in Trinidad circa 2010, serves as a digital means for resurrecting small-town-style communal life, with both the closeness and claustrophobia that this implies. In this sense, Miller argues that it "has reversed two centuries of flight from community" (2011, 181).

It is in this spirit that I wish to conclude by suggesting that social networks have the power to influence or assist precisely the kind of shift in family norms that might make marriage, nonmarital partnership, and diverse arrays of family formation seem more possible, perhaps even desirable, in the Japanese context. They have this ability by virtue of their power to build new assumptions about relationships and interaction into their interfaces and affordances, resulting in new interactional entailments. We could easily imagine making other changes: for example, including women's income on matchmaking profiles. Having this information on the profile could shape the way that matchmakers and their clients search for marriage partners by perhaps encouraging singles to look for someone whose income complements theirs, regardless of gender. Of course, there is no partner matching system with the same kind of scope as Facebook. And while these systems—social media, online dating platforms, matchmaking—are built to serve social interests, they are also designed to serve business interests as well. There is no guarantee that the designers of partner matching services will produce progressive systems that highlight flexibility in relationships, unless there is some market demand for it. Or perhaps, as with the NNK moving to allow male clients with precarious employment to sign up, they will make allowances for greater flexibility in relationship styles when not doing so would be to swim against the strong tide of social change. The phatic systems that any society builds are capable of shaping whole patterns of interaction and relationships. We can hope that the ideas of linguistic perspective-taking and imagination promoted by Japan's matchmakers might become a model for more egalitarian relationships overall. And we can hope that more infrastructural tools are built with a capacious imagination for relationship possibilities. But even equipped with the conceptual and linguistic tools to build out new and more flexible visions of marriage and family in Japan, those families will still need material support.

NOTES

1. Although it bears noting that Tinder introduced a paid "Tinder concierge" service in March 2020 to allow users in some markets to pay for precisely this kind of advice regarding their profiles.

2. Arguably, more could be done to support childbearing outside of wedlock. Hertog (2011) paints a poignant account of unmarried pregnant mothers and their shifting relationships to their natal families as a crucial means of support and survival following their decision to bear children.

3. This is by no means to imply that herbivore men are interested in gay sex—rather, that we simply don't know. Both Ushikubo and Morioka take heterosexuality for granted in their writing, and frame the problem of Japanese millennial masculinity as an inability, difficulty, or reluctance of men to form heterosexual, romantic/erotic relationships with women.

4. John Borneman discusses similar situations in 1990s East and West Germany, in which "legal kinship logic [is] effectively stretched out of recognizable shape" (2006, 34).

Works Cited

Agrawal, Anuja. 2015. "Cyber-Matchmaking among Indians: Re-arranging Marriage and Doing 'Kin Work.'" *South Asian Popular Culture* 13 (1): 15–30. doi: 10.1080/14746689.2015.1024591.

Ahearn, Laura M. 2002. *Invitations to Love: Literacy, Love Letters, and Social Change in Nepal*. Ann Arbor: University of Michigan Press.

Alexy, Allison. 2011. "Intimate Dependence and Its Risks in Neoliberal Japan." *Anthropological Quarterly* 84 (4): 895–917. doi:10.1353/anq.2011.0051.

———. 2020. *Intimate Disconnections: Divorce and the Romance of Independence in Contemporary Japan*. University of Chicago Press. doi: 10.7208/chicago/9780226701004.001.0001.

Allison, Anne. 2012. "Ordinary Refugees: Social Precarity and Soul in 21st Century Japan." *Anthropological Quarterly* 85 (2): 345–370. doi:10.1353/anq.2012.0027.

Alpert, Erika. 2014. "Stoicism or Shyness? Japanese Professional Matchmakers and New Masculine Conversational Ideals." *Journal of Language and Sexuality* 3 (2): 191–218. doi:10.1075/jls.3.2.02alp.

———. 2019. "Miraculous Photos and Beautiful Skin: Roman Jakobson, Semiotic Multifunctionality, and the Art of the Profile Picture." *Semiotic Review 7: Blank Faces*. https://semioticreview.com/ojs/index.php/sr/article/view/37.

———. 2020. "The Role of Dating Site Design in Gendered Self- Representation and Self-Animation in Online Japan." *Journal of Asian Linguistic Anthropology* 2 (4): 67–79. doi: 10.47298/jala.v2-i4-a4.

Aronsson, Anne Stefanie. 2015. *Career Women in Contemporary Japan: Pursuing Identities, Fashioning Lives*. New York: Routledge.

Austin, J. L. 1962. *How to Do Things with Words*. Second Edition. Cambridge, MA: Harvard University Press.

Bakhtin, Mikhail Mikhailovich. 1981. "Discourse in the Novel." In *The Dialogic Imagination: Four Essays*, edited by Michael Holquist, translated by Caryl Emerson and Michael Holquist, 259–300. Austin: University of Texas Press.

Bardsley, Jan, and Laura Miller, eds. 2011. *Manners and Mischief: Gender, Power, and Etiquette in Japan*. Berkeley: University of California Press.

Barrett, Rusty. 1999. "Indexing Polyphonous Identity in the Speech of African American Drag Queens." In *Reinventing Identities: The Gendered Self in Discourse*, edited by Mary Bucholtz, A. C. Liang, and Laurel A Sutton, 313–331. Oxford: Oxford University Press.

Barreto, Amílcar Antonio, and Kyle Lozaon. 2017. "Hierarchies of Belonging: Intersecting Race, Ethnicity, and Territoriality in the Construction of US Citizenship." *Citizenship Studies*, 21 (8): 999–1014. doi:10.1080/13621025.2017.1361906.

Bates, Josiah. "An Alabama Woman Was Charged After Someone Else Killed Her Fetus. Critics Say New Laws Are 'Criminalizing Pregnancy.'" *Time*, July 3, 2019. https://time.com/5616371/alabama-woman-charged-criminalizing -pregnancy/.

Baudinette, Thomas. 2017. "Constructing Identities on a Japanese Gay Dating Site." *Journal of Language and Sexuality* 6 (2): 232–261. doi:10.1075/jls.6.2.02bau.

Bauman, Richard. 2000. "Genre." *Journal of Linguistic Anthropology* 9 (1–2): 84–87. doi: 10.1525/jlin.1999.9.1-2.84.

Befu, Harumi. 2001. *Hegemony of Homogeneity: An Anthropological Analysis of Nihonjinron*. Melbourne: Trans Pacific Press.

Bernstein, Mary. 2006. "The Marriage Contract." In *Handbook of the New Sexuality Studies*, edited by Steven Seidman, Nancy Fischer, and Chet Meeks, 353–359. London and New York: Routledge.

Blood, Robert O. 1967. *Love Match and Arranged Marriage: A Tokyo-Detroit Comparison*. New York: The Free Press.

Boellstorff, Tom. 2008. *Coming of Age in Second Life: An Anthropologist Explores the Virtually Human*. Princeton, NJ: Princeton University Press.

Borneman, John. 2006. "Caring and Being Cared for: Displacing Marriage, Kinship, Gender, and Sexuality." In *The Ethics of Kinship: Ethnographic Inquiries*, edited by James D. Faubion, 29–46. Lanham, MD: Rowman and Littlefield Publishers.

Boyer, Dominic. 2013. *The Life Informatic: Newsmaking in the Digital Era*. Ithaca, NY: Cornell University Press.

Brinton, Mary C., and Eunmi Mun. 2016. "Between State and Family: Managers' Implementation and Evaluation of Parental Leave Policies in Japan." *Socio-Economic Review* 14 (2): 257–281. doi:10.1093/ser/mwv021.

Brown, Penelope. 1998. "How and Why Are Women More Polite: Some Evidence from a Mayan Community." In *Language and Gender: a Reader*, edited by Jennifer Coates, 81–99. Oxford: Blackwell Publishing.

Brown, Penelope, and Stephen C. Levinson. 1987. *Politeness. Some Universals in Language Use*. Cambridge, UK: Cambridge University Press.

Butler, Judith. 1990. *Gender Trouble: Feminism and the Subversion of Identity*. New York: Routledge.

Cameron, Deborah, and Don Kulick. 2003. *Language and Sexuality*. Cambridge: Cambridge University Press.

Carpenter, Morgan. 2016. "The Human Rights of Intersex People: Addressing Harmful Practices and Rhetoric of Change." *Reproductive Health Matters* 24 (47): 74–84. doi:10.1016/j.rhm.2016.06.003.

Carsten, Janet. 1995. "The Substance of Kinship and the Heat of the Hearth: Feeding, Personhood, and Relatedness among Malays in Pulau Langkawi." *American Ethnologist* 22 (2): 223–241.

Chako, Priya, and Kanishka Jayasuriya. 2018. "Asia's Conservative Moment: Understanding the Rise of the Right." *Journal of Contemporary Asia*, 48 (4): 529–540. doi:10.1080/00472336.2018.1448108.

Chodorow, Nancy. 1994. *Femininites, Masculinities, Sexualities: Freud and Beyond.* Lexington: University of Kentucky Press.

Coleman, Gabriella. 2014. *Hacker, Hoaxer, Whistleblower, Spy: The Many Faces of Anonymous.* London and New York: Verso. Kindle edition.

Coltrane, Scott. 2001. "The Marriage 'Solution': Misplaced Simplicity in the Politics of Fatherhood." *Sociological Perspectives* 44 (4): 387–418. doi:10.1525/sop.2001.44.4.387.

Connell, R. W. 2005. *Masculinities,* Second Edition. Berkeley: University of California Press.

Cook, Emma E. 2014. "Intimate Expectations and Practices: Freeter Relationships and Marriage in Contemporary Japan." *Asian Anthropology* 13 (1): 36–51. doi:10.1080/1683478X.2014.883120.

———. 2016. *Reconstructing Adult Masculinities: Part-Time Work in Contemporary Japan.* New York: Routledge.

———. 2019. "Power, Intimacy, and Irregular Employment in Japan." In *Intimate Japan: Ethnographies of Closeness and Conflict,* edited by Allison Alexy and Emma E. Cook, 176–199. Honolulu: University of Hawai'i Press.

Cook, Haruko Minegishi. 2011. "Are Honorifics Polite? Uses of Referent Honorifics in a Japanese Committee Meeting." *Journal of Pragmatics* 43 (15): 3655–3672. doi:10.1016/j.pragma.2011.08.008.

Cornell, Laurel L. 1984. "Why Are There No Spinsters in Japan?" *Journal of Family History* 9 (4): 326–339.

Crook, Jordan. 2015. "Hate It or Love It, Tinder's Right Swipe Limit Is Working." *TechCrunch,* March 12, 2015. https://techcrunch.com/2015/03/12/hate-it-or-love-it-tinders-right-swipe-limit-is-working/.

Dale, S. P. F. 2020. "Same-Sex Marriage and the Question of Queerness—Institutional Performativity and Marriage in Japan." *Asian Anthropology* 19 (2): 143–159. doi:10.1080/1683478X.2020.1756077.

Dales, Laura. 2014. "Ohitorisama, Singlehood and Agency in Japan." *Asian Studies Review* 38 (2): 224–242. doi:10.1080/10357823.2014.902033.

Dalton, Emma, and Laura Dales. 2016. "Online Konkatsu and the Gendered Ideals of Marriage in Contemporary Japan." *Japanese Studies*, 36 (1): 1–19. doi:10.1080/10371397.2016.1148556.

Darling-Wolf, Fabienne. 2003. "Male Bonding and Female Pleasure: Refining Masculinity in Japanese Popular Cultural Texts." *Popular Communication*, 1 (2): 73–88. doi:10.1207/S15405710PC0102_1.

Dore, Ronald Philip. 1958. *City Life in Japan.* Berkeley: University of California Press.

Edin, Kathryn, and Joanna M. Reed. 2005. "Why Don't They Just Get Married? Barriers to Marriage among the Disadvantaged." *The Future of Children* 15 (2): 117–137. doi:10.1353/foc.2005.0017.

Eguchi, Hisashi, Koji Wada, and Derek R. Smith. 2016. "Recognition, Compensation, and Prevention of Karoshi, or Death Due to Overwork." *Journal of Occupational and Environmental Medicine* 58 (8): e313–314. doi:10.1097/JOM.0000000000000797.

Elyachar, Julia. 2010. "Phatic Labor, Infrastructure, and the Question of Empowerment in Cairo." *American Ethnologist* 37 (3): 452–464. doi:10.1111/j.1548-1425.2010.01265.x.

Faier, Lieba. 2009. *Intimate Encounters: Filipina Women and the Remaking of Rural Japan*. Berkeley: University of California Press.

Fukuda, Setsuya. 2013. "The Changing Role of Women's Earnings in Marriage Formation in Japan." *The Annals of the American Academy of Political and Social Science* 646 (1): 107–128. doi:10.1177/0002716212464472.

Fullwood, Chris, Neil Morris, and Libby Evans. 2011. "Linguistic Androgyny on MySpace." *Journal of Language and Social Psychology* 30 (1): 114–124. doi:10.1177/0261927X10387105.

Gagné, Nana Okura. 2020. *Reworking Japan: Changing Men at Work and Play under Neoliberalism*. Ithaca, NY: Cornell University Press. Kindle edition.

Gaudio, Rudolf P. 1994. "Sounding Gay: Pitch Properties in the Speech of Gay and Straight Men." *American Speech* 69 (1): 30–57. doi:10.2307/455948.

Gender Equality Bureau Cabinet Office. 2009. "White Paper on Gender Equality." http://www.gender.go.jp/english_contents/about_danjo/whitepaper/pdf/ewp2009.pdf.

———. 2010. "The Active Participation of Women and Revitalization of Economy and Society." http://www.gender.go.jp/english_contents/about_danjo/whitepaper/pdf/ewp2010.pdf.

Gershon, Ilana. 2010. *The Breakup 2.0: Disconnecting over New Media*. Ithaca, NY: Cornell University Press.

———. 2011. "'Neoliberal Agency'" *Current Anthropology* 52 (4): 537–555. doi:10.1086/660866.

———. 2014. "Selling Your Self in the United States." *PoLAR: Political and Legal Anthropology Review*, 37 (2): 281–295. http://doi.org/10.1111/plar.12075.

———. 2020. "The Breakup 2.1: The Ten-Year Update." *The Information Society* 36 (5): 279–289. doi:10.1080/01972243.2020.1798316.

Giddens, Anthony. 1992. *The Transformation of Intimacy: Sexuality, Love, and Eroticism in Modern Societies*. Stanford: Stanford University Press.

Giles, Howard, and Patricia Marsh. 1979. "Perceived Masculinity, Androgyny and Accented Speech." *Language Sciences* 1 (2): 301–315. doi: 10.1016/S0388-0001(79)80019-4.

Gilhooly, Rob. 2012. "Why Japan Finally Fell in Love with Facebook." *New Scientist* 215 (2875): 20. doi:10.1016/S0262-4079(12)61933-2.

Gist, Noel P. 1953. "Mate Selection and Mass Communication in India." *Public Opinion Quarterly* 17 (4): 481–495. doi:10.1086/266477.

Goffman, Erving. 1959. *The Presentation of Self in Everyday Life*. New York: Anchor Books.

———. 1982. "The Interaction Order." *American Sociological Review* 48 (1): 1–17.

Goldstein-Gidoni, Ofra. 2017. "'The Joy of Normal Living' as the Promise of Happiness for Japanese Women and Their Families." *Asian Studies Review* 41 (2): 280–297. doi:10.1080/10357823.2017.1295021.

Gordon, Andrew. 2017. "New and Enduring Dual Structures of Employment in Japan: The Rise of Non-regular Labor, 1980s–2010s." *Social Science Japan Journal* 20 (1): 9–36. doi:10.1093/ssjj/jyw042.

Gostin, Lawrence O., Wendy E. Parmet, and Sara Rosenbaum. 2020. "Health Policy in the Supreme Court and a New Conservative Majority." *Journal of the American Medical Association.* doi:10.1001/jama.2020.21987.

Gratton, Chantal. 2016. "Resisting the Gender Binary: The Use of (ING) in the Construction of Non-Binary Transgender Identities." *University of Pennsylvania Working Papers in Linguistics* 22 (2): 51–60.

Hall, Kira. 1997. "'Go Suck Your Husband's Sugarcane!': Hijras and the Use of Sexual Insult." In *Queerly Phrased: Language, Gender, and Sexuality,* edited by Anna Livia and Kira Hall, 430–460. Oxford: Oxford University Press.

Hamada, Mayumi. 2012. "A Facebook Project for Japanese University Students: Does It Really Enhance Student Interaction, Learner Autonomy, and English Abilities?" In L. Bradley and S. Thouësny (eds.), CALL: Using, Learning, Knowing, EUROCALL Conference, Gothenburg, Sweden, 22–25 August 2012, Proceedings, 104–110. Dublin: research-publishing.net. doi:10.14705/rpnet.2012.000035.

Hayduk, Ron, and Marcela García-Castañon. 2018. "Xenophobia, Belonging and Agency: Citizenship in Immigrant America." *New Political Science* 40 (2): 309–316, doi:10.1080/07393148.2018.1449936.

Hayes, Anna. 2019. "Interwoven 'Destinies': The Significance of Xinjiang to the China Dream, the Belt and Road Initiative, and the Xi Jinping Legacy." *Journal of Contemporary China* 29 (121): 31–45. doi:10.1080/10670564.2019.1621528.

Hendry, Joy. 1981. *Marriage in Changing Japan: Community and Society.* New York: Routledge.

———. 1992."Honorific as Dialect: The Expression and Manipulation of Boundaries in Japanese." *Multilingua* 11: 341–354.

———. 2017. "Marriage and the Family in Modernising Japan." In *An Anthropological lifetime in Japan: The Writings of Joy Hendry,* 102–122. Leiden: Brill.

Hertog, Ekaterina. 2009. *Tough Choices: Bearing an Illegitimate Child in Japan.* Stanford: Stanford University Press.

———. 2011. "I Did Not Know How to Tell My Parents, So I Thought I Would Have to Have an Abortion: Experiences of Unmarried Mothers in Japan." In *Home and Family in Japan: Continuity and Transformation,* edited by Richard Ronald and Allison Alexy, 91–111. London: Routledge.

Hochschild, Arlie Russell, and Anne Machung. 2003. *The Second Shift.* New York: Penguin Books.

Hollifield, James F., and Michael Orlando Sharpe. 2017. "Japan as an 'Emerging Migration State.'" *International Relations of the Asia-Pacific* 17 (3): 371–400. doi:10.1093/irap/lcx013.

Hommerich, Carola. 2012. "The Advent of Vulnerability: Japan's Free Fall through Its Porous Safety Net." *Japan Forum* 24 (2): 205–232. doi:10.1080/09555803.2012.671842.

Huen, Yuki W. P. 2007. "Policy Response to Declining Birth Rate in Japan: Forma-tion of a 'Gender-Equal' Society." *East Asia* 24 (4): 365–379. doi:10.1007/s12140 -007-9026-8.

Ide, Sachiko. 2004. "Exploring Women's Language in Japanese." In *Language and Women's Place: Text and Commentaries*, edited by Mary Bucholtz, 179–186. Ox-ford: Oxford University Press.

Inoue, Miyako. 2002. "Gender, Language, and Modernity: Toward an Effective History of Japanese Women's Language." *American Ethnologist* 29 (2): 392–422.

———. 2004. "What Does Language Remember? Indexical Inversion and the Naturalized History of Japanese Women." *Journal of Linguistic Anthropology* 14 (1): 39–56.

———. 2006. *Vicarious Language: Gender and Linguistic Modernity in Japan*. Berkeley: University of California Press.

———. 2007. "Language and Gender in an Age of Neoliberalism." *Gender and Language* 1 (1): 79–91.

Irvine, Judith T., and Susan Gal. 2000. "Language Ideology and Linguistic Dif-ferentiation." In *Regimes of Language: Ideologies, Polities, and Identities*, edited by Paul V. Kroskrity, 35–83. Santa Fe, NM: School of American Research.

Ito, Shiori, and Megumi Lim. 2015. "Tokyo Issues Japan's First Same-Sex Partner Certificates." Reuters.com, November 5, 2015. https://www.reuters.com/ar ticle/us-japan-samesex-idUSKCN0SU0MV20151105.

Jakobson, Roman. 1980. "Metalanguage as a Linguistic Problem." In *The Frame-work of Language*, 81–92. Ann Arbor: Michigan Studies in the Humanities.

———. 1990. "The Speech Event and the Functions of Language." In *On Language*, edited by Linda R. Waugh and Monique Monville-Burston, 69–79. Cambridge, MA: Harvard University Press.

Jayal, Niraja Gopal. 2019. "Reconfiguring Citizenship in Contemporary India." *South Asia: Journal of South Asian Studies* 42 (1): 33–50. doi:10.1080/00856401.20 19.1555874.

Jozuka, Emiko, Jessie Yeung, and Jake Kwon. 2019. "Japan's Birth Rate Hits An-other Record Low in 2019." CNN.com, December 30, 2019. https://edition.cnn .com/2019/12/25/asia/japan-birthrate-hnk-intl/index.html.

Kamano, Saori. 2004. "Dokushin Danjo no Egaku Kekkon-Zō [Images of Marriage Depicted by Single Men and Women]." In *Shōshika no Jendā Bunseki [a Gender Analysis of Low Birth Rates]*, edited by Meguro Yoriko and Nishioka Hachirō, 78–106. Tokyo: Keisō Shobo.

Kanai, Atsuko. 2008. "'Karoshi (Work to Death)' in Japan." *Journal of Business Eth-ics* 84 (S2): 209–216. doi:10.1007/s10551-008-9701-8.

Kawasaki, Kyoko, and Kirsty McDougall. 2003. "Implications of Representations of Casual Conversation: a Case Study in Gender-Associated Sentence Final Particles." *Sekai no Nihongo Kyōiku* 13: 41–55.

Keane, Webb. 2007. *Christian Moderns: Freedom and Fetish in the Mission Encounter*. Berkeley: University of California Press.

Keenan, Elinor. 1989. "Norm-Makers, Norm-Breakers: Uses of Speech by Men and Women in a Malagasy Community." In *Explorations in the Ethnography of Speaking*, edited by Richard Bauman and Joel Sherzer, 125–143. Cambridge: Cambridge University Press.

Kelsky, Karen. 2001. *Women on the Verge: Japanese Women, Western Dreams*. Durham, NC: Duke University Press.

Khor, Diana, and Saori Kamano. 2021. "Negotiating Same-Sex Partnership in a 'Tolerant' State." *Journal of Gender Studies*. doi:10.1080/09589236.2021.1929099.

Kiesling, Scott Fabius. 2001. "'Now I Gotta Watch What I Say': Shifting Constructions of Masculinity in Discourse." *Journal of Linguistic Anthropology* 11 (2): 250–273.

Kitaoji, Hironobu. 1971. "The Structure of the Japanese Family." *American Anthropologist* 73 (5): 1036–1057.

Kitzinger, Celia. 2007. "Is 'Woman' Always Relevantly Gendered?" *Gender and Language* 1(1): 39–49.

Kobayashi, Chie, and Julia Hollingsworth. 2021. "Japan's Failure to Recognize Same-Sex Marriage Is 'Unconstitutional,' Court Rules." CNN.com, March 17, 2021. https://edition.cnn.com/2021/03/17/asia/japan-same-sex-marriage-intl-hnk/index.html.

Kondo, Dorinne K. 1990. *Crafting Selves: Power, Gender, and Discourses of Identity in a Japanese Workplace*. Chicago: University of Chicago Press.

Kulick, Don. 1993. "Speaking as a Woman: Structure and Gender in Domestic Arguments in a New Guinea Village." *Cultural Anthropology* 8 (4): 510–541.

———. 1998. *Travesti: Sex, Gender, and Culture among Brazilian Transgendered Prostitutes*. Chicago: University of Chicago Press.

———. 2000. "Gay and Lesbian Language." *Annual Review of Anthropology* 29: 243–285.

Kyodo News. 2021. "Number of Births in Japan Falls to Record Low in 2020." Kyodo News, February 22, 2021. https://english.kyodonews.net/news/2021/02/e06f0b045c90-number-of-births-in-japan-falls-to-record-low-in-2020.html.

Kyoto Prefectural Police. N.d. "Deai-Kei Saito wa Kiken ga Ippai [Dating Sites Are Full of Dangers]." https://web.archive.org/web/20190409121830/http://www.pref.kyoto.jp/fukei/anzen/shonen_s/deai/index.html.

Lakoff, Robin. 1973. "Language and Woman's Place." *Language in Society* 2 (1): 45–80.

Lee, Grace H. Y., and Sing Ping Lee. 2014. "Childcare Availability, Fertility and Female Labor Force Participation in Japan." *Journal of the Japanese and International Economies* 32 (C): 71–85. doi:10.1016/j.jjie.2014.01.002.

Lee, Kristen Schultz, Paula A. Tufiş, and Duane F. Alwin. 2010. "Separate Spheres or Increasing Equality? Changing Gender Beliefs in Postwar Japan." *Journal of Marriage and Family* 72 (1): 184–201. doi:10.1111/j.1741-3737.2009.00691.x.

Lunsing, Wim, and Claire Maree. 2004. "Shifting Speakers: Negotiating Reference in Relation to Sexuality and Gender." In *Japanese Language, Gender, and Ideology: Cultural Models and Real People*, edited by Shigeko Okamoto and Janet S Shibamoto Smith, 92–109. Oxford: Oxford University Press.

Machado, Daniel. 2020. "The Lost Discussion on Sexual Difference in Marriage Law in Prewar Japan." 『社会科学ジャーナル』 *The Journal of Social Science* 87: 109–123.

Malinowski, Bronislaw. 1946. "The Problem of Meaning in Primitive Languages." In *The Meaning of Meaning*, by C. K. Ogden and I. A. Richards, 296–336. New York: Harcourt, Brace, and World, Inc.

McCurry, Justin. 2016. "Japanese Experts Cast Doubt on Poll Linking Sexless Singles to Low Birth Rate." *The Guardian*, September 28, 2016. https://www.theguardian.com/world/2016/sep/28/japan-poll-linking-sexless-singles-to-low-birth-rate-causes-stir.

McElhinny, Bonnie. 1995. "Challenging Hegemonic Masculinities: Female and Male Police Officers Handling Domestic Violence." In *Gender Articulated: Language and the Socially Constructed Self*, edited by Kira Hall and Mary Bucholtz, 217–243. London: Routledge.

———. 2003. "Theorizing Gender in Sociolinguistics and Linguistic Anthropology." In *The Handbook of Language and Gender*, edited by Janet Holmes and Miriam Meyerhoff, 21–42. Malden, MA: Blackwell Publishing.

McLelland, Mark. 2003. "'A Mirror for Men?' Idealised Depictions of White Men and Gay Men in Japanese Women's Media." *Transformations* 6: 1–14. http://www.transformationsjournal.org/wp-content/uploads/2017/01/mclelland.pdf

———. 2010. "'Kissing Is a Symbol of Democracy!' Dating, Democracy, and Romance in Occupied Japan, 1945–1952." *Journal of the History of Sexuality* 19 (3): 508–535. doi:10.1353/sex.2010.0007.

Mesthrie, Rajend, Joan Swann, Ana Deumert, and William L. Leap. 2009. *Introducing Sociolinguistics*. Second Edition. Edinburgh: Edinburgh University Press.

Miller, Daniel. 1998. *A Theory of Shopping*. Cambridge: Polity Press.

———. 2011. *Tales from Facebook*. Cambridge: Polity Press. Kindle edition.

Miller, Laura. 1997. "People Types: Personality Classification in Japanese Women's Magazines." *The Journal of Popular Culture* 31 (2): 143–159. doi:10.1111/j.0022-3840.1997.00143.x.

———. 2004. "Those Naughty Teenage Girls: Japanese Kogals, Slang, and Media Assessments." *Journal of Linguistic Anthropology* 14 (2): 225–247.

Miller, Patrick R., Andrew R. Flores, Daniel C. Lewis, Barry L. Tadlock, and Jami K. Taylor. 2017. "Transgender Politics as Body Politics: Effects of Disgust Sensitivity and Authoritarianism on Transgender Rights Attitudes." *Politics, Groups, and Identities* 5 (1): 4–24. doi:10.1080/21565503.2016.1260482.

Mirza, Vincent. 2016. "Young Women and Social Change in Japan: Family and Marriage in a Time of Upheaval." *Japanese Studies* 36 (1): 21–37. doi:10.1080/10371397.2016.1143331.

Miyamoto Kunihisa and Asami Seo. 2012. *Facebook Koikatsu/Konkatsu: "Omiai" ga Kaeru Atarashii Koikatsu/Konkatsu no Katachi [Facebook Love and Marriage Hunting: The New Shape of Love and Marriage Hunting Created by "Omiai"]*. Tokyo: Magazine House.

Miyazaki, Ayumi. 2016. "Nihon no Chūgakusei no Jendā Ichininshō o Meguru Meta-Goyōteki Kaishaku (Japanese Junior High School Students' Metapragmatic Commentaries: Shifting Gendered Language Ideologies)." *Shakai Gengogaku* 19 (1): 135–150.

Morioka, Masahiro. 2008. *Sōshoku-Kei Danshi no Ren'ai-Gaku [Love-ology for Herbivore Men]*. Tokyo: Media Factory.

———. 2011. "'Sōshoku-Kei Danshi' no Genshō Gakuteki Kōsatsu [Academic Thoughts on the 'Herbivore Man' Phenomenon]." *The Review of Life Studies* 1: 13–28.

Munn, Nancy. 1986. *The Fame of Gawa*. Durham, NC: Duke University Press.

Nakamura, Momoko. 2014. *Gender, Language and Ideology: a Genealogy of Japanese Women's Language*. Amsterdam: John Benjamins Publishing Company.

Nakanishi, Keiji. 2009. *Hajimete no Nakōdo Bijinesu: Seikō no Hikketsu [Your First Matchmaking Business: Success Secrets]*. Tokyo: Gentosha Renaissance.

Nakanishi, Kiyomi. 2012. *Oya no Tame no Kodomo no Konkatsu Ōen Gaido: O-ko-san o Kanarazu Kekkon ni Michibiku Jissen Gaido [Guide for Parents to Support Their Children's Marriage Hunting: A Practical Guide Guaranteed to Lead to Your Child's Marriage]*. Tokyo: Arumat.

Nakano Hitori. 2004. *Densha Otoko [Train Man]*. Tokyo: Shinchosha.

Narayana, Sumthi, Dana Schonberg, Zoey Thill, Jennifer Amico, Allison Paul, and Marji Gold. 2019. "Family Doctors and the Criminalization of Abortion Care." *Family Medicine* 51 (10): 803–805. doi:10.22454/FamMed.2019.731224.

Nardi, Bonnie. 2009. *My Life as a Night Elf Priest: An Anthropological Account of World of Warcraft*. Ann Arbor, MI: University of Michigan Press. doi:10.3998/toi.8008655.0001.001.

National Institute of Population and Social Security Research. 2016. "The Fifteenth Japanese National Fertility Survey in 2015: Marriage Process and Fertility of Married Couples; Attitudes toward Marriage and Family among Japanese Singles; Highlights of the Survey Results on Married Couples/Singles." http://www.ipss.go.jp/ps-doukou/e/doukou15/Nfs15_points_eng.pdf.

———. 2017. "The Fifteenth Japanese National Fertility Survey in 2015: Marriage Process and Fertility of Married Couples; Attitudes toward Marriage and Family among Japanese Singles; Summary of the Survey Results on Married Couples/Singles." http://www.ipss.go.jp/ps-doukou/e/doukou15/Nfs15R_summary_eng.pdf.

Newton, Esther. 1979. *Mother Camp: Female Impersonators in North America*. Chicago: University of Chicago Press.

Nishioka, Hachirō, Toru Suzuki, Yasuyo Koyama, Masato Shimizu, Masakazu Yamauchi, and Keita Suga. 2012. "Household Changes in Contemporary Japan." *The Japanese Journal of Population* 10 (1). http://www.ipss.go.jp/webj-ad/webjournal.files/population/2012_Vol.10Web%20Journal_Vol.10_01.pdf.

Nosaka, Akiko. 2009. "The M-Shaped Dilemma: Life Strategies and Fertility Trends among Working Women in Contemporary Japan." *Ethnology* 48 (1): 21–38.

Nozawa, Shunsuke. 2015. "Phatic Traces: Sociality in Contemporary Japan." *Anthropological Quarterly* 88 (2): 373–400. doi:10.1353/anq.2015.0014.

Obadia, Julienne. 2020. "Introduction: Overwhelmed by Proximity." *Anthropological Quarterly* 93 (1): 1329–1353. doi:10.1353/anq.2020.0014.

Ochs, Elinor. 1992. Indexing Gender. In *Rethinking Context: Language as an Interactive Phenomenon*, edited by Alessandro Duranti and Charles Goodwin, 335–358. Cambridge: Cambridge University Press.

Ochs, Elinor, and Carolyn Taylor. 1995. "The 'Father Knows Best' Dynamic in Dinnertime Narratives." In *Gender Articulated: Language and the Socially Constructed Self*, edited by Kira Hall and Mary Bucholtz, 97–120. London: Routledge.

OECD. 2020. "Hours Worked (Indicator)." https://data.oecd.org/emp/hours-worked.htm doi: 10.1787/47be1c78-en.

Okamoto, Shigeko. 1995. "'Tasteless' Japanese: Less 'Feminine' Speech among Young Japanese Women." In Gender Articulated: Language and the Socially Constructed Self, edited by Kira Hall and Mary Bucholtz, 297–325. New York: Routledge.

Okamoto, Shigeko, and Janet S. Shibamoto Smith, eds. 2004. *Japanese Language, Gender, and Ideology: Cultural Models and Real People.* Oxford: Oxford University Press.

Orgad, Shani. 2009. "Question Two: How Can Researchers Make Sense of the Issues Involved in Collecting and Interpreting Online and Offline Data?" In *Internet Inquiry: Conversations about Method*, edited by Annette N. Markham and Nancy K. Baym, 33–53. Thousand Oaks, CA: SAGE Publications.

Paul, Kari. 2017. "Here Are All the Things Millennials Have Been Accused of Killing—from Dinner Dates to Golf." *MarketWatch*, October 12, 2017. https://www.marketwatch.com/story/here-are-all-of-the-things-millennials-have-been-accused-of-killing-2017-05-22.

Pearce, Celia, and Artemisia. 2009. *Communities of Play: Emergent Cultures in Multiplayer Games and Virtual Worlds.* Cambridge, MA: MIT Press. Kindle edition.

Peirce, Charles Sanders. 1955. "Logic as Semiotic: The Theory of Signs." In *Philosophical Writings of Peirce*, edited by Justus Buchler, 98–119. New York: Dover Publications.

Petersen, Anne Helen. 2014. "How I Rebuilt Tinder and Discovered the Shameful Secret of Attraction." *Buzzfeed News*, September 11, 2014. https://www.buzzfeednews.com/article/annehelenpetersen/we-are-all-classists.

Raymo, James M. 1998. "Later Marriages or Fewer? Changes in the Marital Behavior of Japanese Women." *Journal of Marriage and Family* 60 (4): 1023–1034.

———. 2015. "Living Alone in Japan: Relationships with Happiness and Health." *Demographic Research* 32: 1267–1298. doi:10.4054/DemRes.2015.32.46.

Raymo, James M., and Miho Iwasawa. 2005. "Marriage Market Mismatches in Japan: an Alternative View of the Relationship between Women's Education and Marriage." *American Sociological Review* 70 (5): 801–822.

———. 2008. "Bridal Pregnancy and Spouse Pairing Patterns in Japan." *Journal of Marriage and Family* 70 (4): 847–860. doi:10.1111/j.1741-3737.2008.00531.x.

Raymo, James M., Miho Iwasawa, and Larry Bumpass. 2009. "Cohabitation and Family Formation in Japan." *Demography* 46 (4): 785–803. doi:10.1353/dem.0.0075.

Redmond, Ryan C. 2015. "Bōizu Rabu Manga Ni Okeru Sekushiariti to Yakuwarigo (Linguistic Identity in Japanese Boys' Love Manga)." In *Yakuwarigo/Kyarakutā Gengo Kenkyū Kokusai Wākushoppu 2015 Hōkoku Ronshū (Collection of Papers from the 2015 Workshop on Research into Role Language/Character Language)*, edited by Satoshi Kinsui, 138–150. Osaka: Self-published.

Retherford, Robert D., Naohiro Ogawa, and Rikiya Matsukura. 2001. "Late Marriage and Less Marriage in Japan." *Population and Development Review* 27 (1): 65–102.

Roberts, Glenda S. 2005. "Balancing Work and Life: Whose Work? Whose Life? Whose Balance?" *Asian Perspective* 29 (1): 175–211.

Robertson, Jennifer. 1998. *Takarazuka: Sexual Politics and Popular Culture in Modern Japan*. Berkeley: University of California Press.

Rocha, Pollyanna C. (2018). "Gamification of Love: A Case Study of Tinder in Oslo." MSc Thesis, University of Oslo.

Ronald, Richard, and Allison Alexy. 2011. "Continuity and Change in Japanese Homes and Families." In *Home and Family in Japan: Continuity and Transformation*, edited by Richard Ronald and Allison Alexy, 1–24. London: Routledge.

Ronald, Richard, and Misa Izuhara. 2016. "Emerging Adulthood Transitions in Japan." *Asian Journal of Social Science* 44 (3): 391–415. doi:10.1163/15685314-04403006.

———. 2007. "Robo Sapiens Japonicus: Humanoid Robots and the Posthuman Family." *Critical Asian Studies* 39 (3): 369–398. doi:10.1080/14672710701527378.

Rosenfeld, Michael J., Reuben J. Thomas, and Sonia Hausen. 2019. "Disintermediating Your Friends: How Online Dating in the United States Displaces Other Ways of Meeting." *Proceedings of the National Academy of Sciences* 116 (36): 17753–17758. doi:10.1073/pnas.1908630116/-/DCSupplemental.

Rubin, Gayle. 1975. "The Traffic in Women: Notes on the 'Political Economy' of Sex." In *Toward An Anthropology of Women*, edited by Rayna R. Reiter, 157–210. New York and London: Monthly Review Press.

Sakai, Yūichirō. 2009. "Meiji-Ki 'Baishaku Kekkon' no Seido-ka Katei [The Process of Institutionalization of 'Brokered Marriage' in Meiji Japan]." *Soshioroji* 54: 89–105. https://www.jstage.jst.go.jp/article/soshioroji/54/2/54_89/_article/-char/ja/.

de Saussure, Ferdinand. 1959. *Course in General Linguistics*. Edited by Charles Bally and Albert Sechehaye in collaboration with Albert Riedlinger. Translated by Wade Baskin. New York: McGraw-Hill.

Schoppa, Leonard J. 2010. "Exit, Voice, and Family Policy in Japan: Limited Changes Despite Broad Recognition of the Declining Fertility Problem." *Journal of European Social Policy* 20 (5): 422–432. doi:10.1177/0958928710380477.

———. 2020. "The Policy Response to Declining Fertility Rates in Japan: Relying on Logic and Hope over Evidence." *Social Science Japan Journal* 34 (2): 307–325. doi:10.1093/ssjj/jyz046.

Seppala, Timothy J. 2017. "OKCupid Unveils Major Overhaul to Cull Spam Messages." *Engadget*, August 12, 2017. https://www.engadget.com/2017/12/08/okcupid-messaging-changes/.

Sharpe, Michael Orlando. 2010. "When Ethnic Returnees Are De Facto Guest-Workers: What Does the Introduction of Latin American Japanese Nikkeijin (Japanese Descendants) (LAN) Suggest for Japan's Definition of Nationality, Citizenship, and Immigration Policy?" *Policy and Society* 29 (4): 357–369. doi:10.1016/j.polsoc.2010.09.009.

Shibamoto Smith, Janet S. 2004. "Language and Gender in the (Hetero)Romance: 'Reading' the Ideal Hero/ine through Lovers' Dialogue in Japanese Romance Fiction." In *Japanese Language, Gender, and Ideology: Cultural Models and Real People*, edited by Shigeko Okamoto and Janet S. Shibamoto Smith, 113–130. Oxford: Oxford University Press.

——. 2011. "Honorifics, 'Politeness,' and Power in Japanese Political Debate." *Journal of Pragmatics* 43 (15): 3707–3719. doi.:10.1016/j.pragma.2011.09.003.

Shibamoto Smith, Janet S., and Debra J. Occhi. 2009. "The Green Leaves of Love: Japanese Romantic Heroines, Authentic Femininity, and Dialect." *Journal of Sociolinguistics* 13(4), 524–546.

Shirakawa, Tōko, and Rieko Tada. (2008). *Kekkon Hyōgaki o Norikiru Hon [The Book of Marriage Ice Age Survival].* Tokyo: Media Factory.

Shozo, Shibuya. 2009. *"Konkatsu" no Sahō ["Marriage Hunting" Etiquette].* Tokyo: Tōhō Shuppan Inc.

Siddle, Richard. 2010. "The Limits to Citizenship in Japan: Multiculturalism, Indigenous Rights and the Ainu." *Citizenship Studies* 7 (4): 447–462. doi:10.1080/13621020320000134976.

Silverstein, Michael. 2003. "Indexical Order and the Dialectics of Sociolinguistic Life." *Language and Communication,* 23 (3-4): 193–229. doi:10.1016/S0271-5309(03)00013-2.

Smith, Robert J., and Ella Lury Wiswell. 1982. *The Women of Suye-Mura.* Chicago: University of Chicago Press.

Steiner, Kurt. 1950. "Postwar Changes in the Japanese Civil Code." *Washington Law Review and State Bar Journal* 25: 286–312.

Stokoe, Elizabeth. 2010. "'Have You Been Married, or . . . ?' Eliciting and Accounting for Relationship Histories in Speed-Dating Interaction." *Research on Language and Social Interaction* 43 (3): 260–282. doi:10.1080/08351813.2010.497988.

SturtzSreetharan, Cindi L. 2006a. "Gentlemanly Gender? Japanese Men's Use of Clause—Final Politeness in Casual Conversations." *Journal of Sociolinguistics* 10 (1): 70–92.

——. 2006b. "I Read the Nikkei, Too": Crafting Positions of Authority and Masculinity in a Japanese Conversation. *Journal of Linguistic Anthropology* 16 (2): 173–193.

Sunaoshi, Yukako. 2004. "Farm Women's Professional Discourse in Ibaraki." In *Japanese Language, Gender, and Ideology: Cultural Models and Real People,* edited by Shigeko Okamoto and Janet S. Shibamoto Smith, 187–204. Oxford: Oxford University Press.

Suzuki, Toru. 2006. "Fertility Decline and Policy Development in Japan." *The Japanese Journal of Population* 4(1). http://www.ipss.go.jp/webj-ad/webjournal.files/population/2006_3/suzuki.pdf.

Takeda, Hiroko. 2008. "The Political Economy of Familial Relations: The Japanese State and Families in a Changing Political Economy." *Asian Journal of Political Science* 16 (2): 196–214. doi:10.1080/02185370802204156.

Taylor, Jami K., Daniel C. Lewis, and Donald P. Haider-Markel. 2018. *The Remarkable Rise of Transgender Rights.* Ann Arbor: University of Michigan Press.

Terahara, Makiko. 2021. "Opinion: Japan's Groundbreaking Marriage Equality Ruling Paves the Way for Change." *Washington Post,* March 21, 2021. https://www.washingtonpost.com/opinions/2021/03/20/japan-sapporo-marriage-equality-change/.

Thakor, Mitali, and danah boyd. 2013. "Networked Trafficking: Reflections on Technology and the Anti-Trafficking Movement." *Dialectical Anthropology* 37 (2): 277–290. doi:10.1007/s10624-012-9286-6.

Thomson, Robert, and Naoya Ito. 2012. "The Effect of Relational Mobility on SNS User Behavior: A Study of Japanese Dual-Users of Mixi and Facebook." *Kokusai Kōjō Media/Kankōgaku Jānaru = The Journal of International Media, Communication, and Tourism Studies* 14: 3–22. http://hdl.handle.net/2115/48860.

Tsuda, Takeyuki Gaku. 2001. "From Ethnic Affinity to Alienation in the Global Ecumene: The Encounter between the Japanese and Japanese-Brazilian Return Migrants." *Diaspora: A Journal of Transnational Studies* 10 (1): 53–91. doi:10.1353/dsp.2011.0047.

Twenge, Jean M., Ryne A. Sherman, and Brooke E. Wells. 2017. "Declines in Sexual Frequency among American Adults, 1989–2014." *Archives of Sexual Behavior* 46: 2389–2401. doi:10.1007/s10508-017-0953-1.

United Nations, Department of Economic and Social Affairs, Population Division (2019). "World Population Prospects 2019: Ten Key Findings." https://population.un.org/wpp/Publications/Files/WPP2019_10KeyFindings.pdf.

Upham, Frank K. 2021. "Same-Sex Marriage in Japan: Prospects for Change." *Asian Journal of Comparative Law* 15: 195–224. doi:10.1017/asjcl.2021.2.

Urciuoli, Bonnie. 2008. "Skills and Selves in the New Workplace." *American Ethnologist* 35 (2): 211–228. doi:10.1111/j.2008.1548-1425.00031.x.

Ushikubo, Megumi. 2008. *Sōshoku-Kei Danshi "Ojōman" ga Nihon o Kaeru [Herbivore "Ladymen" Will Change Japan]*. Tokyo: Kodansha.

Vlastos, Stephen. 1998. "Tradition: Past/Present Culture and Modern Japanese History." In *Mirror of Modernity: Invented Traditions of Modern Japan*, edited by Stephen Vlastos, 1–16. Berkeley: University of California Press.

van Vleet, Krista. 2008. *Performing Kinship: Narrative, Gender, and the Intimacies of Power in the Andes*. Austin: University of Texas Press.

Vogel, Ezra. 1961. "The Go-Between in a Developing Society: The Case of the Japanese Marriage Arranger." *Human Organization* 20: 112–120.

Wang, Yilun, and Michal Kosinski. 2017. "Deep Neural Networks Are More Accurate Than Humans at Detecting Sexual Orientation from Facial Images." *PsyArXiv*. September 7. doi:10.31234/osf.io/hv28a.

Ward, Janelle. 2016. "What Are You Doing on Tinder? Impression Management on a Matchmaking Mobile App." *Information, Communication and Society* 20 (11): 1644–1659. doi:10.1080/1369118X.2016.1252412.

Werner, Cynthia. 2009. "Bride Abduction in Post-Soviet Central Asia: Marking a Shift towards Patriarchy through Local Discourses of Shame and Tradition." *Journal of the Royal Anthropological Institute* 15: 314–331. doi:10.1111/j.1467-9655.2009.01555.x

White, Mary Isaacs. 2002. *Perfectly Japanese: Making Families in an Era of Upheaval*. Berkeley: University of California Press.

Yamada, Masahiro, and Tōko Shirakawa. 2008. *"Konkatsu" Jidai [the Age of "Marriage-Hunting"]*. Tokyo: Discover 21.

Yamada, Yumiko. 2008. *Honki de Kekkon Shitai Hito no Omiai Katsudō Manyuaru [Omiai Activity Manual for Those Who Sincerely Desire to Marry]*. Tokyo: Asuka Shinsha.

———. 2009. *Hisshō Konkatsu Mesoddo: "Omiai" to Iu Konkatsu [The Guaranteed Marriage-Hunting Method: Omiai Marriage Hunting]*. Tokyo: Gakken Shinsho.

———. 2012. "Donna Hito o Mōshikondara Ē n?" [What Kind of People Is It OK to Apply to Meet?] http://ameblo.jp/omiai7510/entry-11291174376.html.

Yamaguchi, Tomomi. 2016. "Is There Any Truth to the Portrait of a 'Sexless Japan'?" *International Business Times*, September 21, 2016. https://www.ibtimes.co.uk/there-any-truth-portrait-sexless-japan-1582495.

Zimman, Lal. 2017. "Gender as Stylistic Bricolage: Transmasculine Voices and the Relationship between Fundamental Frequency and /S/." *Language in Society* 43 (3): 1–32. doi:10.1017/S0047404517000070.

Zuckerman, Charles H. P. 2016. "Phatic Violence? Gambling and the Arts of Distraction in Laos" *Journal of Linguistic Anthropology* 26 (3): 294–314. doi:10.1111/jola.12137.

Index

153

of marriage, 70; matchmaker
advice to, 43, 68–69; mediated
contact, 56, 58, 67–68, and *omiai*,
56, 66; and phatic labor, 57–58,
84–85; and problems, according to
matchmakers, 30–31, 67–68; and
profiles, 27–28, 54; success of, 88–90
collective problems. *See* structural
problems
communication, 5–6, 28, 52–53,
55–58, 85–86, 104–105, 134–135;
breakdown of, 85–86; mediated
by matchmakers, 55–56, 67–68;
phatic language and, 16–17, 46–48,
119–120; technologies, 53; and
vulnerability, 57
conservative social values, 10, 13
conversation, 5, 19, 42, 50–52, 58–59,
76, 84–85, 105, 134–135; and app
structure, 56; gender in, 42–43,
45–46, 50; honorifics in, 38; phatic
language and, 46–47; style and
ability, 76; within matchmaking
systems, 55–56; women's
understanding of, 45
counseling, 6–7, 19, 24, 79–80, 84–85,
89, 127–128. *See also* advice

dates, dating, 1, 6, 17, 50, 58–59, 66,
78–79, 84–85, 93–94; choosing an
app, 101–102; cultural flows and,
99; metapragmatics of, 66–67; net
omiai and, 23, 97–98; online and
offline, 115; technology, 107. *See
also* online dating
dating profiles, 5, 25, 27–28, 33–35, 50,
52–55, 57, 76–77, 84, 98–99, 114–115,
119, 133; as a form of social media,
108–9; as genre, 102, 108–112,
114–115; as phatic infrastructure,
48; as phatic technology, 54; as
self-advertising, 5–6; construction
of, 103–8, 128; effects of different
structures of, 134–136; and
matchmaking services, 102;
politeness on, 60, 112–113; profile

photos on, 55, 84, 103–104, 107–108;
variation among, 45, 110–114
dating sites and apps, 27–28, 33–35,
48–49, 54, 56–57, 60, 94–95, 97–103,
119; Japanese perceptions of, 93–94,
95
demographics, 4, 7–10; demographic
crisis, 3–4, 7, 10–11, 16, 120–121,
125; demographic purity, 9;
demographically single, 11
desire, 34, 68–70, 123–124; construction
of heterosexual desire, 122–125;
female desire and agency, 114, 127;
kinship and, 124
divorce, 3, 7, 43, 125, 132

employment, 5, 11–16, 48, 74, 127, 129–
133; dual employment, 14; freeters,
13–14; heteronormative view of, 82,
121; job-hunting (*shūshoku katsudō*),
14; as matchmakers, 81, 88; on
matchmaking databases, 54, 127;
maternity leave, 130–131; relation
to fertility rates, 122; women's
participation in, 131; women's
"second shift," 126
ethnonationalism, 7–10

family, 133; alternative forms of, 2–3,
122–123, 132, 136; and forms of
address in Japanese, 7; economics
of, 126, 130, 136; heteronormative
views of, 9–10, 13, 28, 69–70, 122,
132; Japanese registry system for,
122; role of lifetime employment
system for, 14; roles in the, 7, 133;
women's careers and, 12
femininities, 18, 25; complementarity
with masculinity, 18; cross-
cultural variation among, 36–37;
in language, 36–38, 40, 59; in
matchmaking discourse, 121;
and *ohitorisama*, 11–12; queer and
transgressive forms, 41; in relation
to hegemonic masculinities,
40–41; as shaped by matchmaking

About the Author

Erika R. Alpert is a linguistic and cultural anthropologist who studies gender, sexuality, marriage, and kinship. She received her PhD from the University of Michigan in Ann Arbor in 2014, following five years in Japan researching, teaching, and, effectively, training to be a matchmaker. She has since been based in Kazakhstan at Nazarbayev University in the Department of Sociology and Anthropology. She spends an extraordinary amount of time thinking about connections between Central and East Asia, social media history, and love in all the many forms it takes. She has also written about profile photos, photo manipulation, and honesty; and about the nature of fieldwork as interaction.